PRAEGER REPRINTS ON ARTS,
CRAFTS, AND TRADES

Charles F. Montgomery, General Editor

GEORGE SMITH'S

COLLECTION OF DESIGNS

FOR
HOUSEHOLD FURNITURE AND
INTERIOR DECORATION

WITH A NEW INDEX TO THE 158 PLATES

Introduction by
Constance V. Hershey

Charles F. Montgomery and Benno M. Forman, Editors

PRAEGER PUBLISHERS
New York · Washington · London

PRAEGER PUBLISHERS
111 Fourth Avenue, New York, N. Y. 10003, U.S.A.
5, Cromwell Place, London S.W. 7, England

Published in the United States of America in 1970
by Praeger Publishers, Inc.

Preface, Introduction, and Index © 1970 by Praeger Publishers, Inc.

Library of Congress Catalog Card Number: 69–19362

Printed in the Federal Republic of Germany

EDITOR'S PREFACE

The Newark Museum's outstanding 1963 exhibition, *Classical America, 1815–1845*, focused attention on the character, quality, and beauty of the American arts executed during this thirty-year period. The catalogue of this show provided excellent illustrations and many previously uncollected facts about the exhibition's 290 pieces of furniture, metalwork, ceramics, sculpture, and painting. It also indicated the major sources of inspiration for the design of these works; but, to date, no really satisfactory study of the American furniture of that era has been completed, nor is such a study possible without a serious investigation of the nineteenth-century furniture industry. We need to know much more about shop organization, specialization by craftsmen, working methods, and use of machines. In the absence of a diary or complete shop records revealing the origin of designs, it seems likely that only a photographic census of the popular forms produced in the major centers will make it possible to compare carefully American furniture with English and French design sources.

Without detailed information concerning foreign influence on American cabinetmakers, we must assume that printed sources played an increasingly influential role as the nineteenth century progressed. Of special interest to student and collector alike, therefore, are the works of George Smith of London and Pierre de la Mésangère of Paris. The works of both men appear to have been the major sources of design ideas from abroad. La Mésangère's work is now familiar to us through his *Collection de Meubles et Objets de*

Goût (1802–35). Presumably, his plates made French designs available immediately and directly to interested American cabinetmakers as well as to the French workmen for whom they were published. French furniture was imported into America by Thomas Jefferson, James Monroe, and James Madison, each of whom returned from diplomatic missions to Paris with many cases of French wares.

One might suppose that *émigré* cabinetmakers, such as Antoine Gabriel Quervelle, of Philadelphia, and Charles-Honoré Lannuier, of New York, played significant roles in strengthening the French influence in America. On July 15, 1803, Lannuier advertised in the *New-York Evening Post* that he had: "Just arrived from France, and ... makes all kinds of Furniture, Beds, Chairs, etc., in the newest and latest French fashion; and that he has brought for that purpose gilt and brass frames, borders of ornaments ... as well as new patterns."

While it is true that the terms "French beds" and "French bureaus" were widely used by cabinetmakers in both England and America, direct French influence on cabinetmaking, except in New York and Philadelphia, was slight. The average American cabinetmaker's inspiration came from English sources, and American furniture of the nineteenth century continued to be more English than French, just as it had been in the seventeenth and eighteenth centuries. One could say that the French motifs used by American cabinetmakers had an English accent.

In America, during the first decades of the nineteenth century, probably the most important book of furniture designs was George Smith's A COLLECTION OF DESIGNS FOR HOUSEHOLD FURNITURE AND INTERIOR DECORATION. It apparently appeared in only one edition: All copies known to the editors bear the date 1808. It was published in London by J. Taylor, an ambitious firm that also published the works of Sir John Soane, Humphrey Repton, and James

Stuart and Nicholas Revett. A few of the plates are dated 1806 and 1807, leaving the impression that they were issued separately during those years. The theory that the book was issued in parts is supported by a heading in the introduction, "LIST of PLATES contained in the FIRST PART," and a note at the foot of the same page that reads "The Complete Arrangement of the Plates, with the Descriptions, will be given in the last Part." This idea is further supported by the fact that the plates in this copy were numbered by hand—but in some other copies, engraved numbers appear.

Many of the plates in the copy from which this reprint is taken were hand-colored, although by no means did all copies have this expensive feature. Unlike the line engravings found in most English design books of the eighteenth century, Smith's work consists almost totally of aquatints, which impart a great deal of tonal gradation to the illustrations. This method of reproduction is especially flattering to the representation of textiles.

Although Smith's 1808 *Collection* is seldom encountered in the rare-book market (a copy was recently offered for £300), it can be found in some major museums and art libraries of America and Europe. The 1936 catalogue of the *Staatlichen Kunstbibliothek*, Berlin, lists the book and gives the life dates of Smith as 1782–1869, a piece of information that the editors have been unable to verify elsewhere.

In England, a copy is to be found at the Victoria and Albert Museum. Curiously, it is listed in neither the British Museum catalogue nor its supplement.

In America, there are copies in the library of The Metropolitan Museum of Art, New York; the Library of Congress, Washington, D.C.; and the Library of the Henry Francis du Pont Winterthur Museum, Winterthur, Delaware.

Although John Harris's admirable book *Regency Furniture Designs* (London: Alec Tiranti Ltd., 1961) includes all of the plates greatly reduced in size, the Praeger reprint marks the first time that Smith's COLLECTION has been reissued in its entirety. For the convenience of the reader, a complete index of the plates has been included.

Benno M. Forman
Charles F. Montgomery

INTRODUCTION

A classic misnomer in the vocabulary of the American decorative-arts student is the word "Empire," used to describe the most fashionable furniture and accessories produced in the United States during the first four decades of the nineteenth century. Correctly used, the word refers to a style that had its first popular expression in France around 1800. Except for the work of a few *émigré* French *ébénistes* in New York and Philadelphia, the overwhelming influence in American cabinetmaking was English—just as it had been in colonial times.

In England, the Empire style was popularized by the Whig circle that surrounded the Prince of Wales, later to become the Prince Regent; the term "Regency" is now generally applied to furniture in what was then called the "antique styles."

Nowhere among the numerous books of designs used by English and American cabinetmakers is the form and ornament of early-nineteenth-century furniture better illustrated than in George Smith's A COLLECTION OF DESIGNS FOR HOUSEHOLD FURNITURE AND INTERIOR DECORATION (1808), the book which, according to Ralph Edwards, "standardized the Regency Style." [1]

Smith was an observant reporter and an ingenious adapter. His first book, written between 1804 and 1807, records a wide range of furniture forms, accessories, and ornamental motifs among its 158 plates illustrating 276 separate designs. On the title page, Smith advertises himself as "Upholder Extraordinary to His Royal Highness the Prince of Wales," and cites his designs as being "in the most approved and elegant taste." Speaking of his book as a whole, he states that "the work displays a variety of the newest patterns, combined with classic taste, for the plainest and for the most superb articles of modern furniture, studied from the best antique examples of the Egyptian, Greek, and Roman styles; and to augment this variety, some Designs are given after the Gothic or old English fashion, and also of course the custom of China."[2] The emphasis on Egyptian, Greek, and Roman styles was at the heart of what Smith called "the propitious change which has taken place in our national taste in furniture."

Furniture historians have never agreed on exactly what period of time properly encompasses the "Regency" style in English furniture. Politically, the Regency falls between the years 1811–20 —the decade in which George Augustus, Prince of Wales, ruled for the "old, mad, blind, despised and dying" George III. The influence of the Prince Regent's taste on English culture began, however, much earlier. Brian Reade, in *Regency Antiques* (London, 1953)—perhaps the definitive study of the style—accepted Donald Pilcher's contention that the style spanned the years 1800–30. Reade points out that some furnishings in the "Regency" style were produced both before and after the actual period of the Regency (1811–20). Margaret Jourdain felt that the style was already current at the time Thomas Sheraton published *The Cabinet-Maker and Upholsterer's Drawing-Book* (1791–94); and Clifford Musgrave has pushed the inauguration of the style back to 1784, when Carlton House, the Prince's London residence, was redecorated. He infers that the first work done for the future Regent —the first public manifestation of his tastes—should be taken as the inception.

As Smith stated, the main ingredients of the style are Greco-Roman, with a healthy dash of Egyptian, and—perhaps for patriotism—a measure of more or less "English" Gothic. The sources, synthesized in this successful style, are complex, and to understand fully the end result, one must examine each root by itself.

Before 1760, information about classical artifacts had been limited, for the most part, to knowledge of public monuments. After 1760, the publication of illustrations of artifacts from the buried cities of Pompeii and Herculaneum added significantly to Europe's knowledge of classical architecture, sculpture, and literature. A vast new range of objects was opened to scrutiny—the minutiae of classical man, the useful accompaniments of his private life.

The first man in England to popularize the motifs of these new discoveries was Robert Adam (1728–92). However, Adam merely borrowed ornament from classical sources; he did not adapt classical forms to modern needs. This task was left to designers of the next generation, such as Henry Holland (1746–1806), who, as virtual "architect in residence" to London's Whigs, was the logical choice to receive the Prince's commission (in 1783) to restyle Carlton House in a manner befitting the status of the future George IV.

Sir John Summerson suggests that the immediate inspiration of Holland's design for Carlton House was Rousseau's Hôtel de Salm, completed just a year before Holland's work was begun.[3] It is possible that, while in France, Holland came under the influence of furniture made in the new archaeological style. The influence is clearly present in his drawing—executed around 1788—for a pier table and glass for Woburn Abbey.[4] Indeed, the French character of Holland's furniture was reinforced, because much of it was made in London by *émigré* French *ébénistes*.

The forms and ornamentation of what we call "archaeological classicism," for want of a better term, were already known in England through the work of Giovanni Battista Piranesi, whose *Diversi maniere d'adonare i camini* (Rome, 1769) had been published in an English edition in 1778. However, in order to work from newer and more complete drawings, Holland, in 1794, sent his pupil, Charles Heathcote Tatham (1772–1842), to Rome to sketch classical artifacts. Tatham remained there for two years, and, in 1799, published his own book, *Etchings Representing the Best Examples of Ancient Ornamental Architecture,* a small, but significant, contribution to the new style.

The freshness of "the august simplicity" Holland achieved at Carlton House was admired in its own time by no less perceptive an arbiter than Horace Walpole, who said, "It is the taste and propriety that strike.... How sick we shall be after this chaste palace, of Mr. Adam's gingerbread and sippets of embroidery."[5]

The "antique styles," as distinct from the Adamesque neoclassical designs, seem to have enjoyed their first popularity in post-Revolutionary France, when the furniture makers of Paris were encouraged to develop a style disassociated from that used by the deposed monarchy. The *Directoire* style, which received official encouragement from the governing body whose name it bears, evolved out of Louis XVI forms, to which was applied ornamentation evocative of the ancient Roman Republic. For the French, *Directoire* furniture suggested a likeness between their republic and the ancient republics of Rome and Athens. Examples of this fashion can be seen in illustrated periodicals of that era: *Journal des Dames et des Modes, Tableau Général du Goût,* and *Costumes des Représentants du Peuple.*

The significance of the *Directoire* style, however, lies less in itself than in the fact that it was the foundation upon which Charles Percier (1764–1838) and Pierre-François Fontaine (1764–1853) built the style that was to dominate European and American furniture for almost half a century.

The new style was introduced in 1801, with the publication of Percier and Fontaine's *Recueil des Décorations Intérieurs.* This remarkable book illustrated the main elements that would comprise the Empire style when, three years later, Napoleon became Emperor. Among the novel elements in Percier and Fontaine's book was the introduction of Egyptian motifs, a by-product of Napoleon's expedition, in 1798, to Egypt. The campaign's military success is questionable; its artistic impact is not. Not only was scientific study stimulated by the rediscovery of Egypt, but popular enthusiasm made the Egyptian style of decoration the new exotic "craze" that rapidly replaced the *chinoiserie* of the previous century.

The younger Thomas Chippendale had, in 1804–5, made some pseudo-Egyptian furniture for Stourhead, Wiltshire, and Thomas Sheraton illustrated a few pieces in *The Cabinet-Maker, Upholsterer and General Artist's Encyclopaedia* (1805–6), but the first publication to present the English public with a great many examples of the Egyptian element of the "Regency" style was Thomas Hope's *Household Furniture and Interior Decoration* (1807). Hope seems to have relied upon Baron Vivant Denon's *Voyages dans la Basse et Haute Egypte* (Paris, 1802) as well as Percier and Fontaine's *Recueil;* in addition, he possessed some knowledge of current French furniture.[6] His lavish book included furniture and accessories "after the antique" as well as in the Egyptian style. He was a wealthy gentleman, who, in his youth, had been trained as an architect, and had, thereafter, traveled widely. During his travels, he had amassed an enormous collection of Greek vases and other classical artifacts. Copying furniture forms and ornament from these objects, Hope designed furniture and accessories for his residence, Portland Place, in Duchess Street, London, and his new country home, Deepdene, in Surrey. This furniture and these accessories were constructed to his exact specifications. His scheme of decoration satisfied two objectives: first, to complement his collections with appropriate backgrounds; and, second, to form "the entire assemblage of productions of ancient and modern handicraft, thus intermixed, collectively into a more harmonious, more consistent, and more instructive whole." He also saw his work as an "association of all the elegancies of antique forms and ornaments with the requisites of modern customs and habits...capable of ennobling, through means of their shape and their accessories, things so humble in their chief purpose and destination as a table and a chair, a footstool and a screen."[7]

The range of his forms was narrow, but their effect was startling, even though we can perceive his forms today only through his engravings, which lack the symbolic colors in which each room was appropriately furnished. Hope said that he had sought to recreate

in an accurate and a classic style, that prodigious variety of details and of embellishments, which, under the various characters and denominations of imitative and of symbolic personages, of attributes and of insignia of gods and of men, of instruments and of trophies, of terms, caryatides, griffins, chimaeras, scenic masks, sacrificial implements, civil and military emblems, &c. once gave to every piece of Grecian and Roman furniture so much grace, variety, movement, expression, and physiognomy.[8]

That the "Egyptian Taste" was not designed for every Englishman was plainly stated by Hope:

Let me ... urge young artists never to adopt, except from motives more weighty than a mere aim at novelty, the Egyptian style of ornament... Real Egyptian monuments, built of the hardest materials, cut out in the most prodigious blocks, even where they please not the eye, through the elegance of their shapes, still amaze the intellect, through the immensity of their size, and the indestructibility of their nature. Modern imitations of those wonders of antiquity, composed of lath and plaster, of callico and of paper, offer not one attribute of solidity or grandeur to compensate for their want of elegance and grace, and can only excite ridicule and contempt.[9]

The reaction which Hope anticipated was not long in coming. Sidney Smith, the most famed wit of his day, blasted the book in a contribution to the *Edinburgh Review* of July, 1808. "We do not know," wrote the pundit, "that we have ever met with any thing, out[side] of a newspaper so exquisitely bombastic, pedantic, and trashy as the composition of this colossal volume." He found the designs, "for the most part quite unsuitable for articles of household furniture" because of their bulk, their inconvenience, and their pedantry. "After having banished the heathen gods and their attributes pretty well from our poetry, we are to introduce them habitually into our eating-rooms, nurseries and staircases? . . . Is there any other grown Englishman who would choose to speak of his furniture in this jargon?"

A few attempts were made to copy or adapt Egyptian objects to contemporary use, but the results were aesthetically or functionally disappointing. For most of us today, it is difficult to determine whether a furniture design should be classified as "in the Egyptian style." A stray raven, sphinx, papyrus bud, or hieroglyph decorates many pieces of "Regency" furniture that, in outline and other ornamental details, belong to the dominant Greco-Roman style.

While the Egyptian elements of Hope's designs found scant favor among Englishmen of his time, other aspects of his work exerted tremendous appeal. For craftsmen and designers, the starkness of Hope's lines invited variation and elaboration; the relationship between ornamented and bare surfaces heightened an already renewed interest in the possibilities of wood as an element of design. Needless to say, the popularity of bulky furniture throughout the nineteenth century had its origin in Hope's work, and, accordingly, disproved Sidney Smith's prediction that Hope's designs would be roundly rejected.

Hope's archaeologically accurate drawings in *Household Furniture* were perhaps too stringent for public and cabinetmaker alike. They needed to be softened in order to become usable. This process is nowhere better illustrated than in the way George Smith treated the same motifs in his A COL-LECTION OF DESIGNS FOR HOUSEHOLD FURNITURE AND INTERIOR DECORATION.

Smith's first book has been characterized by no less astute a commentator on English furniture than Edward T. Joy as "the most comprehensive pattern book of the time."[10] The style reveals a high degree of assurance. More to the point, the furniture and accessories were designed with the capabilities of the average English cabinetmaker in mind. There can be no question that the availability of well-designed objects for the cabinetmaker to copy both encouraged the production of furniture in the style and resulted in a uniform element in the objects produced at this time. Thus, the book may be seen not only as a prime force in popularizing the style, but also as as a mark indicating the beginning of its high period. As Brian Reade points out, every book which illustrates "Regency" furniture exhibits pieces of which Smith must be considered the "editor," though not the author. Reade presents a concise list of the motifs which Smith popularized. They include: lion monopodia used in pairs or groups (Plates 83 and 87); lion-paw feet, frequently with wings (Plates 76, 111, and 117); fan-shaped anthemion brackets (Plates 33, 49, and 63); and tables whose pillars rise from folded lotus buds (Plate 69).

In the introduction to his third book, *The Cabinet-Maker and Upholsterer's Guide* (1826), Smith claimed to have had "an experience of forty years devoted to the study of cabinetmaking, upholstery, and drawing both in theory and practical application." If we can accept Smith's word—and we must, for virtually no other biographical information on him exists—this would mean that his working life began around 1786. Although Smith, in 1826, at approximately age sixty-five, still described himself as an "Upholsterer and Furniture Draughtsman to His Majesty," he may not have been very actively engaged in furniture making, for he also informs us that he was then "Principal of the Drawing Academy," in Brewer Street.[11]

It is ironic that, thus far, no surviving furniture has been documented as actually coming from Smith's shop, although Nancy V. McClelland, in *Duncan Phyfe and the English Regency* (New York, 1939), illustrates a chair and a cabinet (Plates 5 and 6) that, because of their close similarity to the forms in *Designs for Household Furniture,* might well have originated there.

Smith's status as a tradesman may never be ascertained. His influence as a designer, however, indicates that, in his time, he was held in high esteem. For example, Richard Brown, the author of *The Rudiments of Drawing Cabinet and Upholstery Furniture* (1822), ranks "Mr. Smith's excellent book of Unique Designs" with "Mr. Hope's mythological work [and] Percier's splendid French work" as exponents of the Grecian style.[12]

Also obscure are the sources of Smith's designs. It is probable that, in the tradition begun by Thomas Chippendale, Smith was reporting on both what was being imported from France and what was being made in London. If we consult the published sources available to Smith between 1804 and 1807, when the drawings for the book were being engraved, it becomes clear that Smith was gifted with the ability and good taste to combine elements from these sources into effective new designs. The speed with which design motifs were assimilated into actual works at this time is well illustrated by Thomas Hope's complaint of the "extravagant caricatures [of my designs] such as of late have begun to start up in every corner of this capital, [which] seem calculated for the sole purpose of bringing this new style into complete disrepute."[13]

Perhaps Smith was the very man of whom Hope complained; many of Smith's designs are strongly reminiscent of Hope's drawings. A careful comparison of their works, however, reveals significant differences as well as some obvious similarities. Hope was, after all, a scholar, an archaeologist, and an antiquarian. The plates in his book, and, indeed, the furniture in his homes, reveal a rather literal translation of antique stone furniture and forms into wood. Smith, however, used the "antique" as a means rather than an end. While Hope almost invariably makes the form of the object merely comply with the ornament, Smith strives to integrate the form and ornament into an effective piece of furniture. Hope's general tendency is toward geometrical solidity. Smith's designs are confections of his fancy; and, for example, when one looks at a chair made from one of them, it is apparent that form and ornament are wedded brilliantly.

Elements of the new style, however, were well known to London cabinetmakers before either Hope or Smith's publications appeared. The inclusion of "Grecian" front and back legs and "Grecian backs" (with illustrations) in the 1802 *London Chair-Makers' and Carvers' Book of Prices* is conclusive evidence that Greco-Roman elements were being used in English furniture at that time; this book of "Prices for Workmanship" covers only those styles generally current in the trade. By the time the 1808 *Supplement* was published, the list included Grecian couches, Roman and Grecian chairs, chairs with Grecian cross fronts, "Trafalgar Chairs" (a variant of the *klysmos* chair), Egyptian chairs, and Grecian claw legs.

A COLLECTION OF DESIGNS FOR HOUSEHOLD FURNITURE AND INTERIOR DECO-RATION is essentially a catalogue of illustrations; its short Preface and Preliminary Remarks serve as commentary rather than instruction. Smith contents himself, for the most part, with brief descriptions of the plates, indicating rooms in which the furniture may be used and recommending appropriate fabrics for the upholstery. Some comments are hardly more than expanded captions; most provide a terse paragraph or two of description; a few burst into vigorous condemnation of the misuse of one style or expatiate on the grandeur of another.

The "antique" mode, as one might expect, is given most space and is presented in greatest variety. Two hundred and three of the book's 276 designs illustrate furniture and accessories in a Greco-Roman style. Chairs, "chaises longues," stools, and tables were adapted, respectively, from *klysmoi,* Roman couches, folding stools, and tripods retrieved from classical sites or copied from paintings on antique pottery. To the ancient forms, he added an inventiveness that is the true measure of a designer's ingenuity. His "classical" chiffoniers, cellarets, *escritoires,* sideboards, jardinieres, and other accoutrements of late-Georgian living would have astounded the citizens of Athens, Rome, and Thebes.

Although classical and classically-derived designs constitute slightly more than 73 per cent of DESIGNS FOR HOUSEHOLD FURNITURE, Smith also illustrated furniture and interiors in the Gothic, Egyptian, and Chinese styles. He advised that the last was "highly improper and out of taste" (that is, out of style) except "where grandeur and show are necessary." It may be presumed that his caveat also applied to the other exotic styles.

A comment in Rudolph Ackermann's *Repository* (May, 1810) that "no person of a genuine taste will introduce articles in [the Gothic] style into his apartments, unless there be a general correspondence in the appearance of his house" echoes Smith's earlier admonition that "Great care should be taken in fitting up apartments [in the Gothic style] to adopt an uniformity of ornament, and not to introduce any melange of dates and styles." However, although Smith exhorted others to maintain consistency in design, he was not above placing an Egyptian dressing glass atop a Roman bench (Plate 127), or setting caryatids in the form of Egyptian priests to support the top of a pier commode surmounted by Greco-Roman acroteria (Plate 115).

Twenty-eight designs illustrate Smith's conception of the Gothic mode, and its motifs are never mixed with those of other styles and ages, as if he were anticipating the sacrosanct quality of what would be classified as "the only native old English style." Smith partially expressed this notion when he commented that the style was "applicable only for a real gothic mansion; if otherwise used, it would be highly improper and out of taste."

Smith's Gothic seems to stand in spirit, as it does in time, somewhere between the frivolous and whimsical eighteenth-century" Rococco-Gothic" of Horace Walpole's "Strawberry Hill," and the measured earnestness of Augustus Charles Pugin's reverential and reforming Gothic of the 1830's. Cusped arches, crockets, trefoils, and quatrefoils are all present in Smith's designs, and admirably convey the spirit (if not the substance) of authentic detail. Their modernity is betrayed by the application of Gothic ornament to forms that were unknown in the Middle Ages, such as the sofa table in Plate 85, a masterpiece of incongruity, and a Gothic cylinder desk and book case (Plate 100).

Judging from surviving examples, Smith's Gothic seems to have been his least successful group of designs. A revival of this style lay in the future. From the year in which DESIGNS FOR HOUSEHOLD FURNITURE was issued until August, 1825, Ackermann's *Repository* printed only one plate showing

"Gothic" furniture.[14] With the publication of A. C. Pugin's "Gothic Lamp for a Hall," in 1825, the vogue may properly be said to have begun; every piece of furniture illustrated in the next twenty-four numbers of that magazine was in the Gothic style.

In Smith's DESIGNS FOR HOUSEHOLD FURNITURE, seventeen plates have motifs that are clearly derived from Egyptian sources, and several others show Egyptian decoration applied to objects primarily Greco-Roman in inspiration. Apparently, Smith sensed that the Egyptian was best handled as an accent; its large architectural shapes could be most successfully adapted to large "Regency" forms, such as the wall-filling decorative panel in Plate 145 and the library book case in Plate 102. Both of these designs show that most of Smith's knowledge of Egyptian art came from architectural sources.

Undoubtedly, Smith and other designers breathed a sigh of relief when the vogue for the Egyptian proved short-lived. Ackermann wrote a painless obituary for the style in the August, 1809, issue of the *Repository:*

> It cannot but be highly gratifying to every person of genuine taste, to observe the revolution which has, within these few years, taken place in the furniture and decorations of the apartments of people of fashion. In consequence of this revolution, effected principally by the study of the antique, and the refined notions of beauty derived from that source, the barbarous Egyptian style, which a few years since prevailed, is succeeded by the classic elegance which characterized the most polished ages of Greece and Rome.[15]

Smith's prefatory remark promising inclusion of the Chinese "custom" may have been prompted by habit, for only eight illustrations in that worn-out style are to be found in his book: Plate 3, a Chinese cornice; Plate 81, two tea tables; Plate 149, the fireplace wall of a drawing room; and several Chinese frets, added, rather perfunctorily, to Plate 158. The Chinese mode had, after more than a century, lost a great deal of its exotic appeal. The enlightened eighteenth century regarded the East with intense curiosity and admiration. "*Chinoiserie* offered a limitless and beguiling garden in which each could make his own delicious discoveries or revisit the familiar revelations of some professional guide."[16] By 1800, however, the East had surrendered most of its mystery and much of its fascination. Although the Royal Pavilion at Brighton, brilliantly renovated between 1815 and 1822 by John Nash, epitomizes the exotic taste of the Regency, it is, in fact, the final, sumptuous efflorescence of Orientalism.

The Prince Regent may have given the initial impetus to the new style in the social circle he dominated, but the excesses of the Brighton Pavilion (carried out at public expense), combined with the declining popularity of the man who became, after 1820, King George IV, curtailed further emulation. Margaret Jourdain has noted a contemporary remark that, perhaps, summarizes the normal attitude of Englishmen to the last of the Georges: "C. B. Wollaston, who saw Windsor Castle in 1828 noticed the 'dazzling splendour of the gilding, which seems to be much overdone,' and Mr. W[yatt]ville said it was 'His Majesty's taste.'"[17] Although Smith dedicated his book to His Royal Highness, the Prince of Wales, his own sentiments (rather than those of the Prince), expressed in the Preface, are more indicative of trends that furniture design and manufacture were to take in the next half-century. "The dissemination of such designs...[is necessary so that] the beauty and elegance displayed in the fittings-up of modern houses may not be confined to the stately mansions of our nobility in the metropolis, but be published for the use of the country at large."

Constance V. Hershey

NOTES

1. *The Shorter Dictionary of English Furniture* (London, 1964), p. 680 (hereafter cited as *Shorter Dictionary*).

2. Preliminary Remarks, p. vii.

3. *Georgian London* (New York, 1946), p. 132 (hereafter cited as Summerson).

4. Peter Ward-Jackson, *English Furniture Designs of the Eighteenth Century* (London, 1958), Fig. 302.

5. Summerson, p. 133.

6. In the caption to Plate XXIV, No. 3, Hope notes that metal on mahogany chairs "at Paris . . . have been carried to a great degree of elegance and perfection."
   Thomas Hope, *Household Furniture and Interior Decoration* (London, 1808), p. 35 (hereafter cited as Hope).

7. *Ibid.* pp. 3—4, 7.

8. *Ibid.* p. 9.

9. *Ibid.* p. 27.

10. *The Country Life Book of Chairs* (London, 1964), p. 74.

11. *Shorter Dictionary*, p. 680. The great attention paid in this latter book to the mechanics of perspective drawing, etc., suggests that Smith had, indeed, cultivated an academic bent.

12. p. x.

13. Hope, p. 12.

14. "Fashionable Furniture," III, facing p.393

15. *Ibid.*, p. 392.

16. *Ibid.* II, 132.

17. *Regency Furniture, 1795—1830* (London, 1965), p. 13.

INDEX TO PLATES

_____

All numbers refer to plates. Letters indicate order of designs on plate from left to right, top to bottom.

XXVIII

Pl. 1.

Drawing Room Window Cornices.

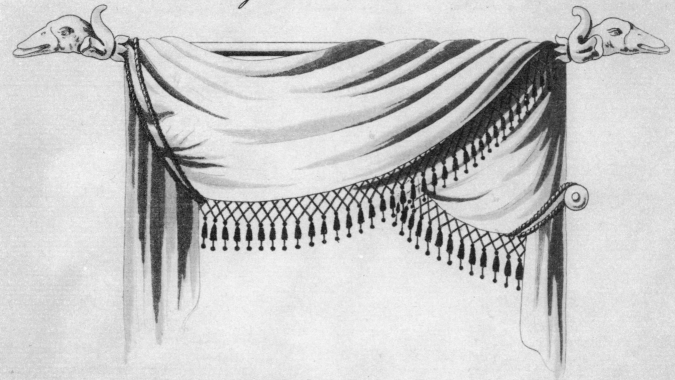

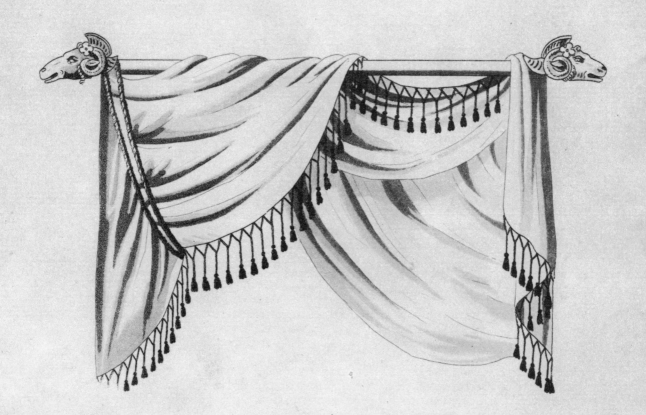

London, Published July 1. 1805, by J. Taylor, No. 59, High Holborn.

A

COLLECTION OF DESIGNS

FOR

HOUSEHOLD FURNITURE

AND

INTERIOR DECORATION,

IN THE MOST APPROVED AND ELEGANT TASTE;

VIZ.

Curtains ; Draperies ; Beds ; Cornices ;
Chairs and Sofas for Parlors, Libraries, Drawing Rooms, &c. ;
Library Fauteuils ; Seats ; Ottomans ; Chaises Longue ;
Tables for Libraries, Writing, Work, Dressing, &c. ;
Sideboards ; Celerets ; Bookcases ; Screens ; Candelabri ; Chiffoniers ;
Commodes ; Pier Tables ; Wardrobes ; Pedestals ; Glasses ;
Mirrors ; Lamps ; Jardiniers ; &c.:

WITH

VARIOUS DESIGNS FOR ROOMS, GEOMETRICAL AND IN PERSPECTIVE,

SHEWING THE DECORATIONS, ADJUSTMENT OF THE FURNITURE, &c.

ALSO

SOME GENERAL OBSERVATIONS,

AND

A DESCRIPTION OF EACH PLATE.

ENGRAVED ON 158 PLATES, FROM ORIGINAL DRAWINGS.

BY GEORGE SMITH,

UPHOLDER EXTRAORDINARY TO HIS ROYAL HIGHNESS THE PRINCE OF WALES.

LONDON:
PUBLISHED BY J. TAYLOR, AT THE ARCHITECTURAL LIBRARY, NO. 59, HIGH HOLBORN.
1808.

S. GOSNELL, Printer, Little Queen Street.

PREFACE.

The taste and fashion in Furniture, and in the decorative parts of modern houses, have lately undergone so great a change, that an apology is not necessary for introducing this work to the public. The superb style in which Household Furniture, particularly the upholstery part, is now executed, and the classic elegance which guides the forms of Cabinet-work, render a publication of Designs on so important and costly a part of modern embellishment absolutely necessary, that the beauty and elegance displayed in the fittings-up of modern houses may not be confined to the stately mansions of our Nobility in the metropolis, but be published for the use of the country at large, as a guide to foreign nations, and as an evidence of the superior taste and skill exhibited in the manufactures of this country.

Change in fashion becomes a source of wealth and commerce, and contributes to those daily occupations which make life preferable in civilized society, and, when founded on true taste, should be encouraged with all possible care, as well by the Virtuoso as by the true Patriot. I must here beg leave to congratulate my countrymen on the propitious change which has taken place in our national taste of Furniture: this has arisen from a more close investigation and imitation of the beautiful remains of ancient sculpture and painting, which have been studied by enlightened travellers, and also been laid before the public in various books of great cost and elegance.

To His Royal Highness the Prince of Wales the highest praise is due, who has so liberally employed his elegant fancy and acknowledged good taste in promoting this noble pursuit after classic originals : and the elegant display of superior *virtù* exhibited in his palaces in Pall Mall and at Brighton, at the same time it evinces an enlightened and highly cultivated mind, has not failed of exciting many noble persons to follow so laudable an example ; and I am happy to say, that a corresponding taste and liberality has been shewn by various gentlemen of high rank, who have lately exercised the most liberal encouragement of the best artists in the different departments concerned in the embellishments of modern houses.

I cannot here do a better service to my brother artists, than by recommending them to study, with all care and assiduity, the numerous examples which may be selected from various antique specimens of sculpture and painting, which may be seen in the Galleries and Libraries of the curious : it is only by a minute observation of apparently the most trifling parts, that the studious artist becomes habituated to compare, to select, and to arrange ; taking not so much the mere pattern or imitation, but the spirit and principle on which the original was composed : hence will arise new forms and combinations in an endless variety, still keeping the original in view, according to the abilities of the designer and the skill of the workman.

It must be observed, that the enlightened artist can only find suitable encouragement under the fostering care of men of large fortune and liberal minds ; and I am happy to say that scarcely any article for domestic use, possessing beauty of form or elegance of workmanship, but has been bought with a liberality and eagerness, which shews more want of able artists than of liberal patrons.

In selecting the articles and in composing the Designs for this work, I have been anxious to exhibit principally such as are suitable to elegant and polite life, and for adorning the most extensive mansion as well as the social villa: and I flatter myself the work displays a variety of the newest patterns, combined with classic taste, for the plainest and for the most superb articles of modern furniture, studied from the best antique examples of the Egyptian, Greek, and Roman styles; and to augment this variety, some Designs are given after the Gothic or old English fashion, and also according to the costume of China.

How well I have succeeded in adopting, in the following Designs, the maxims and precepts which I have recommended to others, is not for me to say: yet I cannot but feel myself highly flattered in seeing so many of my inventions carried into execution by different workmen, and in having been myself employed by some of the most exalted characters in the country to manufacture many of the Designs, some of which have been considered the most difficult to be executed.

G. S.

LIST of the PLATES.

A

PRELIMINARY REMARKS.

THE following Designs are arranged under the two principal features of the business, viz. the Upholsterer's Work, and the Cabinet-maker's Work; and, previously to a description of each Plate, I shall offer a few remarks, which will, I trust, be considered both just and useful. The young artist, I must suppose, has attained sufficient knowledge of perspective and drawing to sketch any subject his eye may see, his fancy invent, or his employer suggest; for, without an early attention to the imitative art, his hopes of attaining to eminence in his profession must be considerably abated.

I shall consider the Upholder's Work under the general title of

DRAPERY.

In no part of his profession is the English Upholsterer more deficient than in the arrangement and in the forms of his Draperies, which arises entirely from the want of an attentive observation of what is easy and elegant: from this deficiency of knowledge, we often see silk and calico tormented into every other form than agreeable, natural Drapery. The mystery and difficulty of *cutting-out* would vanish, did the artist but apply his mind with resolution to conquer his established prejudices: to the workman very little knowledge is requisite beyond cutting-out what is usually called a festoon, the arrangement, whether for continued Drapery or for a single window, forming the principal difficulty; one festoon, well and properly cut out, will answer for the whole: this difficulty once overcome, a little ingenuity will readily accomplish whatever else may be required.

I must here observe, for the guidance of the workman, the utter impossibility of forming tasteful and well-flowing Draperies of the stiffened materials at present in general use; it is nearly as practicable to throw buckram into easy and graceful Drapery, as the modern high-glazed stiffened calicoes: the stiffening must be dispensed with, or the utmost effort of the artist will be in vain. The pleasantest materials are silk and fine cloth.

It may be proper here to mention the various sorts of materials used for the different descriptions of Curtains: for Eating Rooms and Libraries, a material of more substance is requisite than for Rooms of a lighter cast; and for such purposes superfine cloth, or cassimere, will ever be the best; the colours as fancy or taste may direct; yet scarlet and crimson will ever hold the preference: undressed morine may be substituted for cloth, although it does not suit for every description of drapery: calico when used should be of one colour, in shades of moroon or scarlet.

In elegant Drawing Rooms, plain coloured satin or figured damask assumes the first rank, as well for use as for richness: lustring and tabarays the next; the latter, however, makes but indifferent drapery. Calico, the next in choice, and of so great variety of patterns, should, where good drapery is required, be glazed mellow: the small chintz patterns hold a preference in point of effect, especially for draperies. Salisbury flannel has been much used, but is of too slight a quality for curtains of large dimensions.

The arrangement of Drapery for the different descriptions of apartments will ever be subject to the control of fancy; Dining Rooms and Libraries being simple and plain in their decorations, require less variety in the drapery for their curtains. What is commonly called Roman drapery, and which in fact is taken from the Roman standards, may generally be adopted : a tasteful variety of forms lies entirely in the skill of the artist employed. For specimens I refer to Plates 2, 5, 6, 8, 10, 11, 12, 13.

For the decoration of elegant Drawing Rooms, the continuation of festoons, called continued drapery, holds a preference, the arrangement of which may be seen in Plates 1, 2, 4, 12, 13, 153. But as the decorations of almost every room will admit of change in form, and the great difference of windows may also require an essentially different arrangement, the artist will have ample opportunity of displaying his taste and fancy according as circumstances may direct, by a proper choice and combination of the various patterns here laid before him.

OF CABINET-MAKER'S WORK.

I have much pleasure in declaring, that in the operative parts of cabinet-work, the workmen of England excel those of every other country in the accuracy and precision of the joiner's part, which is truly admirable. The artisans of France, attentive more to exterior effect, have attended principally to forms, and what relates to outline; and herein they certainly have attained pre-eminence.

It is to be regretted, that our higher class of artists do not give their attention, in some degree, to providing our manufacturers with patterns of tasteful outline for this species of furniture: their previous course of study, aided by a reference to books of antiquities, would enable them to supply Designs, which in execution would produce a pleasing effect, and merit the just praises of true taste.

In France the first-rate painters do not think themselves degraded by providing Designs for the Cabinet-maker or for the Upholsterer.

Why should they ? Why should not our moveable furniture possess elegance, and give as much pleasure to the eye, as pictures or any other embellishment appropriated to the same apartment ?

I have great pleasure in declaring, that very extensive and liberal encouragement has of late been given by our Nobility and Gentry to various artists employed in manufacturing cabinet-work, the good effects of which will, I doubt not, soon be felt in bringing forward a supply of able workmen, and in promoting an increase of skill and taste in their several departments: for as the beauty of the Antique consists in the purity of design, and what was pleasing centuries ago continues to be equally so now; so I do not despair of seeing a style of Furniture produced in this country, which shall be equally agreeable centuries hence.

The following practical observations on the various woods employed in cabinet-work may be useful. Mahogany, when used in houses of consequence, should be confined to the Parlor and Bedchamber Floors ; in furniture for these apartments the less inlay of other woods, the more chaste will be the style of work : if the wood be of a fine, compact, and bright quality, the ornaments may be carved clean in the mahogany : where it may be requisite to make out pannelling by an inlay of lines, let those lines be of brass or ebony. In Drawing Rooms, Boudoirs, Anti Rooms, or other dressed apartments, East and West India satin-woods, rose-wood, tulip-wood, and the other varieties of woods brought from the East, may be used: with satin and light-coloured woods the decorations may be of ebony or rose-wood : with rose-wood let the decorations be *or molu*, and the inlay of brass : bronzed metal, though sometimes used with satin-wood, has a cold and poor effect ; it suits better on gilt work, and will answer well enough on mahogany.

DESCRIPTIONS OF THE PLATES.

PLATE 1.—*Drawing Room Window Cornices.*

THESE Draperies for Drawing Rooms should be made of satin or lustring, with under-curtains of muslin or superfine cassimere; the fringe, silk, &c. of one colour, in contrast with the drapery. The Cornices gold, without any mixture of bronze. Such Curtains should never be less than six feet in breadth, where it will admit.

PLATE 2.—*Window Cornices and Drapery.*

These Draperies are also intended for Drawing Rooms, and should be made of silk, to have a rich effect; or else of fine cassimere; and in both cases bordered with black velvet. The fringe on the second Design may be formed of two colours, of which there should be two shades in each, provided the contrast is not too strong. The Cornices would look best in entire gold, matt and burnish; or if variety is required, the ornaments may be matt gold, and all the ground imitation of bronze.

PLATE 3.—*Cornices and Drapery in the Chinese Style.*

The Designs in this Plate are calculated for apartments decorated wholly in the Chinese style, where grandeur and show are necessary; in which case the Curtains should be made wholly of silk or velvet, and in either case embroidered with yellows to imitate gold. The Cornices partly japanned, the rest in burnished or matt gold. These Curtains would have a very good effect in calico for secondary rooms: the grounds a dark green, and the ornaments of deep yellow.

B

PLATE 4.—*Window Cornices,* A.

The Cornices on this Plate are according to the Etruscan style, and are copied and coloured from antique fragments. This class of Cornice will answer for secondary rooms, where magnificence is not so much required; in which case the draperies may be of plain coloured calicoes, or small chintz patterns, and the fringe of worsted; the Cornices partly gilt and partly japanned in suitable colours.

PLATE 5.—*Window Curtain,* D.

This Design, after the Egyptian style, is proper for Dining Rooms or Libraries, and should be made of superfine cloth, scarlet or crimson; or, where expense is an object, undressed morine of a fine quality, will form a good substitute. This Cornice is intended to be part japanned; the heads carved and in bronze: the fringe should be of two colours opposed to the cloth, and will answer extremely well in worsted; the pattern on the drapery is drawn by hand.

PLATE 6.—*Window Curtain,* B.

This Curtain is proper for Morning Rooms or Boudoirs: the Draperies and Curtains may be of plain calicoes, with borders cut out in velvet, brown and green, and neatly sewed on; the fringe of worsted finely worked. A muslin Curtain is fixed on one side, to be drawn across the window during the time the sun shines or the light being too strong. The architraves of such rooms should be ornamented with carved work or painted, and crowned with an ornament instead of a Cornice.

PLATE 7.—*Window Curtain,* C.

Is calculated for Breakfast Parlors, and may be made of cloth or morine; the fringe of worsted; the Cornice and cloak-pins of carved work, in imitation of bronze.

PLATE 8.—*Window Curtain, A.*

This Curtain is appropriate only to rooms of consequence, and should be wholly of satin or damask, with an under Curtain of muslin, and a worked ornamental raised border bound with silk: the satin Curtains and Drapery to be bordered with velvet, cut out and neatly sewed on; the Cornice finished in bronze and gold.

PLATE 9.—*Military Window Curtain,*

Is appropriated to Dining Rooms or Libraries: the material may be of fine scarlet cloth, or morine undressed; the ornament on the vallens to be printed in black, and a similar border on the Curtains; the spears supporting the whole to be of mahogany and bronze, or gilt and bronzed.

PLATE 10.—*Continued Drapery and Window Curtains, A.*

Continued Drapery is suitable to Venetian, Bow, or large Windows; the materials may be of plain-coloured or printed calicoes; the Curtains to draw on rods after the French manner, and the Draperies suspended from an ornamental Cornice, which may be executed in gold and bronze; the fringe in silk and cotton. In Bow Windows the centre Curtains may hang down, as shewn in the Drawing.

PLATE 11.—*Continued Drapery and Window Curtains, B.*

This Design is for a Continuation of Drapery over Windows and Piers in one line, which imparts a grand and magnificent effect to a room: this may be made of superfine cloth, or undressed morine, and will answer either for Dining Room or Drawing Room.

PLATE 12.—*Continued Drapery,*

Suitable for a Drawing Room having two windows, and should be of silk, with rich fringe of the same; a muslin Curtain to each window,

4

to draw on rods as usual. Curtains thus constructed require spring blinds of the same colour as the principal Draperies, to drop behind the muslin, and the Drapery to remain as fixed. The enrichments for the Cornice may be carved and gilt, or bronzed, &c.; the Drawing shews the Pier Glass and Table, behind which is a Glass to the floor.

PLATE 13.—*Continued Drapery,*

Proper for a Bow, having three windows, and may be finished agreeably to the foregoing description: the Drapery to remain fixed, and the Curtains to draw on rods as usual.

PLATE 14.—*Bed Pillars,*

Shews four Designs, which may be of mahogany carved, or satin-wood, with ornaments carved and bronzed, or japanned. Where the rails are carved, the bases must be tacked to slips fixed under them.

PLATE 15.—*Bed Pillars, with Foot-board,* A.

Design for Bed Pillars with Foot-board, and shews the arrangement for fixing the bases, as described before.

PLATE 16.—*Bed Pillars, with Foot-board,* B.

Agreeable to the preceding Plate. The Pillars are supposed of satin-wood, inlaid with ebony.

PLATE 17.—*Bed Cornices,* B.

Cornices and Draperies for elegant Beds, which may be of silk or calico, the colours at pleasure.

PLATE 18.—*Bed Cornices in the Gothic Style.*

Two Designs in the Gothic taste, and adapted particularly to houses where this style prevails in the interior. Such work should be wholly in gold, or in English oak, the ornaments and mouldings gilt: in state apartments, the furniture and vallens to such Beds require to be of velvet or fine cassimere, with embroidered borders, and trimmed with rich deep silk fringe.

PLATE 19.—*Cribb Bedstead.*

Design for a Cradle Bed, in the Gothic style, suitable to many mansions in this country: should be of mahogany or oak, the enrichments carved, either plain or gilt; the furniture cotton or silk. This construction of Cradle Beds is of general use, and applicable to the simplest forms and ornaments.

PLATE 20.—*Tent Bed.*

The furniture calico, and trimmed with worsted or cotton fringe at pleasure.

PLATE 21.—*Field Bed.*

The furniture of plain or printed calicoes; the border cut out in black Manchester velvet, and sewed on.

PLATE 22.—*Design for a Bed,* B.

This Design in the rustic style is suitable to a cottage or country residence; the furniture as usual; the pillars and rails may be selected from rough materials, cleaned and varnished.

PLATE 23.—*Military Officer's Bed.*

Design for a French Bed standing under a canopy, partaking of the military character, and raised on a platform; the furniture may be of yellow calico, lined with blue, the vallens blue, lined with yellow, the war trophies carved and bronzed.

PLATE 24.—*Design for a Dome Bed.*

The furniture may be of calico or silk, the exterior green, and linings yellow; the foot curtains are divided four feet from the ground, and fixed at the top, the curtains drawing each way as required ; the head curtains should be full, to meet the foot curtain, the head cloth to be gathered in large plaits.

PLATE 25.—*Design for a Bed,* **A.**

A Design for a Dome Bed, with straight cornices and plain antique vallens ; the curtains to be looped up on the outside of the posts; the head board is stuffed and covered, to answer the exterior, in plaits similar to those in the head cloth : the furniture may be of crimson, lined with yellow, the bases and counterpane also yellow.

PLATE 26.—*Design for a Bed.*

Design for a State Bed : the tester is coved inside, and supported by mahogany pillars and figures carved and gilt; the bedstead is after the French style ; the furniture should be of lilac silk, embroidered border and lining, with rose-coloured Persian ; the counterpane the same ; the outside of the cove may be japanned or velvet painted ; the ornaments and cornice gilt and bronzed.

PLATE 27.—*Polonaise Bed.*

The dome of this Design is circular, with an octangular tester ; the inside divided into compartments with painted ornaments, or quilled with silk or cotton ; the curtains of rich silk, yellow, and lined with blue, or crimson velvet, lined with garter blue silk ; the fringe and tassels of gold. The exterior of the dome, the vallens, and coverlid, to be of the same colour and material as the lining : the carved work should be gilt and bronzed. This style of Bed is calculated only for apartments of state and elegance.

PLATE 28.—*State Bed.*

There is no kind of work better calculated to produce a grand effect, so far as relates to furniture, than what is usually called Gothic, as is shewn in the present Design, admitting of a more abundant variety of ornaments and forms than can possibly be obtained in any other style: and as many of the mansions of our Nobility and Gentry are at this time finished in a similar taste, this Design may not be deemed unacceptable.

It is proper this description of furniture should be elevated above the floor, on a platform of two or three steps, which should be covered with carpet or cloth of an even single colour, adapted as circumstances may require, to accord well with the bedstead; which, if executed in gold, will admit of some of the heavier colours, and if in oak, the colours must be of a lighter cast.

Beds of this kind, from their expense, are confined to few individuals, but are highly in character in the mansions of our Nobility or Gentry, opulent through a long line of ancestry: the present Design is therefore well calculated to exhibit the different inter-marriages on the shields distributed throughout the exterior of the bedstead. The pillars which support the canopy are intended to be of open work the whole height above the pedestal, inclosing a wrought iron pillar adorned with ornaments in character. The curtains should be made of Genoa velvet, satin, or superfine cloth, a suitable border being worked round them on an embroidery of gold; the ground also of the tester must be of the same material and colour as the curtains, on which the carved work is laid, producing a splendid appearance. This species of Bed does not admit of drapery; the rods, &c. supporting the curtains are concealed between the outside and inside cornices. Within the canopy is placed the bedstead, suitably carved and decorated; the bedding consists wholly of mattresses, is covered with a velvet counterpane, pannelled out, and richly embroidered with gold.

The various ornaments of this Design should be well studied previously to being executed; and if correctly outlined, the carving also being well performed, the appearance will be not only pleasing but grand. It is needless perhaps to add, this style is applicable only in a real

Gothic mansion; if otherwise used, it would be highly improper and out of taste.

PLATE 29.—*French Bed.*

The tester with the dome is attached to the wall, and supports the curtains, which draw round the bedstead, which is in the form of a sofa. The furniture may be of rich materials as before described, such beds being calculated for elegant apartments.

PLATE 30.—*French Bed for a Recess.*

In the daytime this Bedstead, being low, for sitting on, is drawn into the room, and used as a couch; the frame-work is usually of mahogany, with the ornaments bronzed; the Recess is lined with calico, in antique drapery.

PLATES 31 and 32.—*French Bed and Wardrobe.*

This Design is suitable only to apartments of the greatest elegance; the Bedstead stands in a recess, which is lined with silk or calico, in large flutes, with antique drapery as a vallens; the ceiling coved and painted in colours to answer the linings; the coverlid, of which two Designs are shewn, may be of figured muslin, laid on a coloured silk; the frame-work of the Bedstead mahogany, with bronzed ornaments, standing on a platform; the curtains, which draw before the Bed, are of rose-coloured silk with black velvet border on a yellow ground; the outside vallens straw colour, and trimmed with deep silk French fringe; the recesses on each side the Bed are fitted up as Wardrobes; the upper pannels of the doors are looking-glass, the whole decorated with carved therm figures, and the moldings and ornaments *or molu* and bronze.

PLATE 33.—*Bed Steps.*

These Designs are made of mahogany or satin-wood, with the ornaments bronzed, and are suitable only to elegant chambers: the Steps should be covered with carpet.

PLATE 34.—*Hall Seats for Recesses.*

These are made of beech-wood, carved and japanned to imitate marble and bronze.

PLATES 35 and 36.—*Hall Chairs and Sofa.*

Mahogany will ever be a wood in general use for Chairs dedicated to the use of halls; their backs as well as seats are generally solid; but where the pattern is Gothic, and the backs partly cut through, oak is used with great propriety; the arms on the shield being emblazoned in proper colours: these kind of frames may also be executed in beech-wood and japanned stone colour, the moldings, &c. relieved in greys.

PLATES 37 and 38.—*Parlor Chairs.*

In mansions professedly Gothic these Chairs are the most appropriate, and should be made of brown oak varnished; the seats may be stuffed or have loose cushions, and in both cases covered with leather, the colour of no great consequence: mahogany is not to be recommended for this kind of work, which requires wood of a close and tough grain, being in places greatly undercut.

PLATES 39 and 40 A. *Parlor Chairs.*

The frames of these Chairs should be made of bright Spanish mahogany, the ornaments partly carved, and partly inlaid with ebony; or the ornaments may be executed with good effect, if inlaid with brass; the seats French stuffed, and finished in red morocco leather, on the border of which may be printed a Grecian ornament in black; over the heads of the tacks may be put a molding of brass, or of dyed wood in imitation of ebony.

PLATE 41.—*Library Seats.*

The frames may be of mahogany or gilt, the seats of leather, and the mantle of cloth.

PLATE 42.—*Library Chair with Desk and sliding Footstool.*

These Chairs are used chiefly in Libraries of some extent, seeing they require to be made of large dimensions to obtain a good effect of outline as well as ease, when used for study ; there cannot be a better material than mahogany for chairs, where bronze is likewise introduced, this colour harmonizing very well with such wood ; the seats may be covered with leather, either stuffed to the frame, or used with cushions. The Desk attached to these Chairs is formed two ways : it may be fixed to the side of the elbow, and capable of elevation by means of a rack and spring ; at the same time, acting on a centre, it can be used in all directions : another mode is, the Desk is fixed on the top of the stump or elbow of the Chair, and, although incapable of elevation, is equally useful, as acting on a centre similar to the former. This article should always be accompanied with a Stool as a rest for the feet, when used for reading or writing.

PLATES 43 C, 44 A, 45 B, and 46 D.—*Library Chairs.*

The frame-work of these Chairs is usually made of mahogany or any elegant wood, the carved ornaments gilt or bronzed, the seats and backs of morocco leather or velvet, according to fancy.

PLATE 47.—*Library Fauteuil.*

This article, which is of French invention, and adapted only to an elegantly furnished Library, is made very deep (two feet six inches) in the seat ; a stand for a lamp and another for books usually accompany this piece of furniture, of which one should be on each side the fireplace ; the whole stands on a platform in imitation of marble ; the materials as before described.

PLATE 48.—*Library Fauteuils in Profile.*

Two Designs, to which the foregoing remarks are applicable.

PLATES 49 and 50 B.—*Footstools.*

Twelve Designs for Footstools, suitable to Parlors, Drawing Rooms, &c.; the frames may be of mahogany, gold, or bronze, and covered with leather, velvet, or printed cloth, suitable to the apartment.

PLATE 51.—*Tête-à-tête Seats.*

An article adapted to elegant apartments; the frames of rich wood, or gold and bronze; the covering of fine cloth, velvet, or calico; in dimension, it is calculated for two persons to sit on.

PLATE 52.—*Window Seats.*

PLATE 53.—*Drawing Room* X *Seats.*

The description to Plate 51 will answer to these Plates. The three last articles are intended as ornamental and extra Seats in elegant Drawing Rooms. See the Design and Description of a Drawing Room at the end.

PLATES 54, 55, 56 C, 57, and 58.—*Drawing Room Chairs.*

Chairs for Drawing Rooms admit of great taste and elegance as well as variety, and are constructed of rich and costly materials in accordance with the room; the frames of satin-wood, burnished gold, with parts of bronze, or otherways highly enriched; the seats covered with silks, painted satins, painted velvets, superfine cloth, or chintz. The Designs on Plate 54 in the Gothic style, as well as several of the others, are proposed to be elegantly carved and finished in matt and burnished gold.

PLATES 59 and 60.—*Sofas.*

Three Designs for Sofas, intended for Libraries, the frames of which should be of mahogany; or they may in part be bronzed, the covering of leather or cloth, with ornamental borders printed.

PLATES 61 and 62.—*Drawing Room Sofas.*

Two Designs calculated for first-rate houses, the frames of which should be all gold, or gold with bronzed ornaments; the covering of satin, silk, or velvet: the latter will admit of ornamented borders, painted in water-colours, and produce a very superb effect.

PLATES 63, 64 A, 65 B, and 66.—*Chaise Longue.*

Four Designs for *Chaises Longue*, an article admissible into almost every room. The present Designs are intended for Drawing Rooms, or Boudoirs, in which case the frames may be of satin-wood, inlaid with other woods, and the ornaments of bronze, as Plates A and B; or in gold, with bronzed ornaments, as Plates 63 and 64. For covering, silks or cloth may be used; and in more moderately furnished apartments calico may suffice, provided the pattern be small and of the chintz kind. The same Designs will answer extremely well for Libraries, Parlors, or Dressing Rooms, executed in mahogany, and divested of the ornaments.

PLATES 67 and 68.—*Ottomans.*

Two Designs of Ottomans for Galleries, which should be placed on the chimney side of the room, with similar seats on the opposite side: the frames may be of mahogany, with ornaments bronzed or carved clean in the wood; or they may be japanned to imitate bronze, and the ornaments in gold. Where show is designed, the covering should be of superfine cloth, or chintz-pattern calico; the fringe worked in fine worsteds. Ottomans are particularly useful in Picture Galleries, their projection from the wall preventing the pictures being fingered, which is too often practised.

PLATE 69.—*Dining Table.*

This Design is intended to do away the necessity of claw feet, and will answer as well for sets of Dining as for single Tables. A rim, two inches in depth, is fixed all round under the top, which adds considerably to their solidity. These Tables will cost considerably more than those of the old form, but possess advantages over them, where large projecting claws are a great inconvenience.

In Fig. 1, the top remains fixed on the pillar, and does not turn up as is usual. The casters are contained in a brass case, concealed in the plinth.

Fig. 2 and 3 are on a lighter construction, and turn up as usual. The parts in line shew the block with a pin, on which the top turns: there is likewise a molded frame under the top, which conceals the block and clamps. The plinths are quadrangular on the plans, as shewn in Fig. 4.

PLATE 70.—*Harlequin Table.*

This elegant article, an appendage to the Ladies' Boudoir. is so contrived, as to form a Writing, Work, Drawing, and Breakfast Table, as occasion may require.

For the first purpose, a small Escrutoire, concealed in the body of the Table, rises by springs, a writing flap rising also in front; the drawer on the right hand of the Table containing the ink, pens, &c. The centre drawer is fitted up with the necessary apparatus to the Work Table. The left hand drawer is fitted up with the colours and other useful articles for Drawing. The two ends of the Table, forming flaps, are supported by lopers thrown forward by springs, when the flaps are raised up parallel with the top, making this article serve as the Sofa or Breakfast Table. The lopers are secured back by spring catches when the leaves are required to be put down.—This piece of decorative furniture should be made of rose-wood, the ornaments of real *or molu,* for the sake of durability; or it may be made of mahogany, and the ornaments of bronzed metal : the top should be covered with morocco leather, divided into pannels by gilt ornamental bordering, which will serve to conceal the joints made necessary in the top by the rising Escrutoire.

PLATE 71.—*Gentleman's Dressing Table.*

This article should be made wholly of mahogany, without any inlaid or carved ornaments. The cupboard in the centre part is meant for boots and shoes; above are two drawers for linen, as are also the drawers in the left wing; the upper drawer in the right wing being fitted up with a variety of dressing apparatus.

PLATE 72.—*Dressing Tables.*

These Tables are intended for the piers in Ladies' Dressing Rooms, and contain five drawers in each, without any dressing apparatus; the ornaments are formed by an inlay of ebony, or carved in the mahogany; casters are concealed in the feet: the drawers, without handles, are locked with spring catches, and released by springs behind.

PLATE 73.—*Ladies' Dressing Table.*

This piece of furniture, and the Design following, are adapted only for decorated apartments, and to accompany State Bedchambers. The present Design, if made of mahogany, may have all the ornamental parts carved in lime-tree and bronzed, or carved in the mahogany with the rest of the Table: should rose-wood be preferred, the whole of the ornaments may be finished in gold. The centre of the top, as likewise the folding tops on the two sides, should be covered with leather, purple or red, with a border of gold: the standards of the Glass screw in and out at pleasure by a nut underneath, in which case the Table will answer as a Sofa Writing Table, the drawer in the centre part being fitted up with writing apparatus.

PLATE 74.—*Ladies' Dressing Table and Glass.*

This Design may be manufactured in mahogany or oak, the moldings and ornaments in gold, or of black rose-wood; the balls of ivory; the top, as in the preceding Plate, covered with leather. The top of the centre divides, and slides under the end tops, uncovering a tray fitted up for dressing apparatus; the drawers, on each side the bason drawer, contain water bottles, boxes, &c. The Glass accompanying this Design is intended to be placed on the Table, and contains three drawers.

PLATES 75, 76, and 77.—*Work Tables.*

These articles of furniture should be made to imitate bronze and gold, with parts of antique marble. In Plate 75 the top should be covered with morocco leather, under which is a drawer for writing apparatus; casters are concealed under the plinths. The Work-bag in Plate 76 may be lustring or satin, round which is suspended a silk fringe. In Plate 77 the tops may be executed in *scagliola*, the edges secured by an *or molu* rim.

PLATE 78.—*Backgammon Work Table.*

This ornamental piece of furniture will admit of every variety in execution; and, where expense is not an object, the whole frame may be gold, and the ornaments in bronze. The inside must be covered entirely with leather, to prevent noise, when used for play. The ends contain concealed drawers, which hold the chess and backgammon men. The casters are concealed in the plinths, supporting the whole.

PLATE 79.—*Tea Poys, Quartetto Tables, and Canterburies.*

Tea Poys and Quartetto Tables are used in Drawing Rooms, &c. to prevent the company rising from their seats when taking refreshment. The Canterburies are intended for holding such music-books as are in constant use. All these articles may be manufactured in mahogany, rose-wood, or bronzed and gilt, to suit the different rooms they may be placed in.

PLATE 80.—*Screen Writing and Work Table.*

The Design in this Plate would answer best in gold and bronze; the bag of velvet or satin; the screen of the same: the drawer contains writing apparatus. Rose-wood would not be an improper material for this Table; but mahogany should be avoided, as least proper for elegant Drawing Rooms. Wainscot may be used, provided the whole fitting up of the room is of a same material.

PLATES 81 and 82.—*Dejuné Tables.*

These Tables, adapted for a breakfast set of superb china, are used for Ladies' Boudoirs or Morning Breakfast Rooms, and therefore partake of the richest decoration. Those in the Chinese taste may be finished in green and gold, red and gold, or blue and gold, agreeable to the style of china placed on them. If used in rooms slightly decorated, they are made to imitate bamboo, or japanned black and gold. In Plate 82 the Table should be wholly made to imitate *or molu,* the top and plinth being of *scagliola,* to imitate red porphyry : the border round the top of *or molu.*

PLATES 83 A, 84 B, and 85.—*Sofa Tables.*

These Designs form furniture for the Drawing Room, Breakfast Parlor, or Library, and should be manufactured in mahogany, rose, or satin woods, and may be in part carved and bronzed, or gilt; the tops in the centre part sometimes slide out, and conceal a backgammon or chess board. Plate 85 will not answer so well in mahogany as other woods : the cushion under, at the time it gives strength to the Table, forms a rest for the feet, and should be covered with velvet ; the foot-stool partakes of the same finishings.

PLATES 86, 87 B, 88 C, and 89.—*Library Tables.*

These Tables may be made of mahogany or other woods, as fancy dictates, and be covered with morocco leather or cloth. In Plate 86, the ornamental part of the drawers is intended as an inlay of ebony ; the heads in metal, answering as handles as well as screening the keyholes ; the chimeras may be carved in wood and bronzed. The same observations apply to the other Designs. Plate 87 shews a rising Desk in the middle.

PLATE 90.—*Dumb Waiters.*

These Designs, though Gothic, will admit of being made of mahogany, having less open work than some of the preceding Designs in this style; they would look extremely well in wainscot, darkened to imitate old oak. The rims round the shelves will answer best to be made of metal, pale lacquered, to imitate *or molu.*

PLATE 91.—*Legs for Sideboards.*

The observations on the following Plates, containing Designs for Sideboards, will apply to these six Designs, which offer a variety suitable to most occasions.

PLATES 92 A, 93 B, 94 C, and 95 D.—*Sideboards.*

These articles of so general use can scarcely be made of any other wood than mahogany, in which case the ornaments in bronze will have a good effect : Sideboards may each contain three drawers, for holding napkins, &c. One of the pedestals in Plates 92 A, 93 B, and 95 D, is lined with tin, with racks to hold plates, which are kept hot by an iron heater: the other pedestal should have a tray capable of holding six or eight bottles, which turns on a centre ; also a drawer under, containing water to wash glasses during dinner. The figures holding lights are of plaster bronzed. Plate 94 C, being without pedestals, has a wine cooler under it, which must be lined with lead.

PLATE 96.—*Pedestals for Sideboards.*

The above remarks apply to these Designs.

PLATE 97.—*Celerets and Wine Cistern, in the Gothic Style.*

These pieces of furniture should be made of wainscot, varnished dark to imitate oak, in preference to using mahogany, for which this style of work is not so well suited. These articles should be lined with lead, if meant to contain water.

D

PLATE 98.—*Celerets.*

Mahogany will answer best for these Designs, the ornaments of which may be carved and bronzed; the interior finished as before directed. These pieces of furniture have all of them casters concealed in the plinths.

PLATE 99 A.—*Bookcase.*

This Bookcase would look well executed in rose-wood, the therm figures and pedestal carved and gilt in matt gold; or, if manufactured in satin-wood, the figures and pedestals being bronze would have an equally good effect: if mahogany is preferred, the less contrast that is used the better; the whole being kept in one wood produces a pleasing and solid appearance.

PLATES 100 and 101.—*Bookcases in the Gothic Style.*

The preceding observations may apply for these, excepting that there is no necessity for gilding any part of them. These two Designs contain a gentleman's wardrobe in each. The upper doors may be backed with lustring in flutes, if it is required to screen the books. This article of furniture, though in the Gothic style, may with great propriety be executed in mahogany.

PLATE 102.—*Library Bookcase.*

This Design is calculated for an extensive Library, where it can be carried round three sides of the room, and would answer best made of mahogany, in which case the ornaments may be of ebony inlaid; the figures in imitation of bronzed metal.

PLATE 103.—*Library Bookcase, with Wings and Secretaire.*

This piece of furniture, after the Gothic taste, may be manufactured, with good effect, in mahogany or oak. Under the Secretaire drawer is a wardrobe concealed with folding doors. The two Wings may contain drawers for linen, making this article very serviceable in a Gentleman's Library or Morning Room.

PLATE 104.—*Dwarf Library Bookcase.*

Literature and the fine arts going hand in hand, this kind of Bookcase is well adapted to the connoisseur in sculpture and painting; nevertheless, such Bookcases can only be applied with propriety in rooms on a large scale, and in Libraries of considerable extent. From the lowness adopted in the present Design, the walls remain free for paintings; at the same time, figures or antique sculpture, placed this height before the spectator, will afford the most pleasing appearance in galleries of any extent. This sort of Bookcase, finished on each side alike, and placed one at each end, centrically, in the room or gallery, with a Library Table between them, produces a grand and pleasing effect. In this Design mahogany alone should be used, and of the finest quality, free from any inlaid work; the ornamental parts to be carved, and finished to imitate bronze.

PLATE 105.—*Dwarf Bookcase.*

This Bookcase answers every purpose of the preceding; and being moderate in design, can be more generally adopted, especially where elegance does not become an essential requisite.

PLATES 106 and 107.—*Bookcase Doors.*

The first Plate contains three styles of design, Chinese, Egyptian, and Gothic; the second Plate, wholly fancy. Each of these Designs may be executed in woods or metal, and may be used with or without glass in the pannels, at pleasure; the doors having curtains of silk, to slide on rods, as occasion may require.

PLATES 108 and 109 B.—*Screens.*

These articles of general use admit of every species of decoration; viz. of entire gold, bronze and gold, or japanned; of mahogany, rose, or satin wood; as the apartment they may be destined for shall require. The mounts, if expense be not regarded, may be carved solid in wood, and embellished with painted decorations; or painted on silk or velvet. Where the stands are wholly mahogany, the mounts may be covered with lustring in flutes, with tassels to suit.

PLATE 110.—*Drawing Room Cheval Screens.*

The Designs in this Plate are appropriate for Drawing Rooms, to be executed wholly in carved work and gilt, and varied with bronzed ornaments on a gold ground. If manufactured of mahogany, the frames may have the ornaments made out in an inlay of ebony, the carved parts in bronze, real, or carved in wood; the mounts of satin, lustring, or velvet, as occasion may require. This kind of Screen answers extremely well for Dining Rooms, made plain of mahogany, with frames to slide out on the sides, covered with plain coloured stuff.

PLATE 111.—*Tripod Stands, &c.*

These stands may be carved in lime-tree, and bronzed to imitate metal, or wholly gilt, agreeable to the rest of the furniture of the apartment they may be intended for. In addition to their use, as stands for Screens and Tables, they are calculated to form elegant supports for music-desks.

PLATE 112.—*Candelabri,* B.

This article of furniture, the Designs of which have been taken from antique examples in the King of Naples' collection, are used as stands for Candlesticks and Lamps, and are serviceable to stand at the corners of Card Tables, or on each side of Couches, or in the angles of rooms, staircases, &c. When used for lamps, they answer for staircases or halls of extent; in galleries, whether for antiques or pictures, these Designs will always have a classic effect.

PLATE 113.—*Candelabri,* A.

The Designs in this Plate are adapted for the angles of Drawing Rooms, or state apartments, to support silver Candlesticks, smaller Candelabri, or transparent alabaster vases, with lights inside. They may be executed, where elegance is required, wholly in gold, or partly in imitation of bronzed metal.

PLATES 114 and 115.—*Chiffoniers.*

In almost every apartment of a house these articles will be found useful, whether decorated or plain; their use is chiefly for such books as are in constant use, or not of sufficient consequence for the library: on the same account they become extremely serviceable in libraries, for the reception of books taken for present reading. The most simple are manufactured in plain mahogany, or japanned in imitation of various woods; the more elegant in mahogany, with decorations in imitation of bronze metal: rose-wood and gold come under similar recommendation, and gold with bronzed ornaments, where expense is not an obstacle.

PLATE 116.—*Book-shelf and Brackets.*

Over a Console Table, in the pier between windows, this kind of Book-shelf is perfectly appropriate; and with silvered plate glass between the brackets would have a good effect. In point of finishing, what has been said of Chiffoniers will answer equally to these. The Brackets accompanying this Design are intended to support lights, clocks, &c. to be executed in gold, or bronze and gold, as may suit best the rooms.

PLATE 117.—*Drawing Room Commodes.*

These Commodes are intended for those Drawing Rooms used also as living rooms, and have therefore doors to screen or secure such articles as may be placed in them: they may be made of satin-wood, rose-wood, or in gold on a white ground, or japanned in imitation of the finer woods; the tops either real marble, or japanned in imitation.

22

PLATE 118.—*Commodes.*

These two Designs are intended for Ladies' Dressing Rooms, where a superior style of elegance in furnishing is adopted; they may be made of the finest rose-wood or mahogany; in the first the whole of the decoration should be executed to imitate *or molu*; in the latter, a mixture of gold and bronze would have a good effect.

PLATE 119.—*Commode for Drawing Room.*

This article may be executed in rose-wood or mahogany, and should be placed in an apartment of consequence; its situation is opposite the chimney, which should also correspond to it in form; the glasses over each producing a most charming effect. This piece of furniture would make an elegant case for an organ, to be placed at the extremity of a long apartment or gallery.

PLATE 120.—*Pier Table and Glass.*

What has been said in explanation of the foregoing Design in regard to situation may be applied to this, the chimney opposed to it partaking of the same design; it may be executed in rose-wood or mahogany, and decorated with gold or bronze after the manner we have before recommended, and as shewn on the Plate. The Glasses over these Designs, as well as the Chimney Glass, should not have any ornament as head pieces, but be carried quite to the cornice of the room.

PLATE 121.—*Console Tables.*

PLATE 122.—*Drawing Room Pier Table.*

These Tables, the decoration of apartments of consequence, cannot be too well attended to in the manufacture, their beauty consisting greatly in the execution and proper conception of the parts, ornamented with chimeras; the Table may be rose-wood, or in imitation of marble; the whole of the decoration in matt gold, of even execution, to produce a solid and metal-like appearance; or mahogany may be used, if the same material is otherways introduced in the apartments, in which case the decorative parts may be finished in imitation of bronzed metal; a silvered plate of glass is placed at the back, the pier being filled also with looking-glass above the book-shelf.

PLATES 123 and 124.—*Escrotoire.*

This piece of furniture belongs chiefly to the Ladies' dressing room, or boudoir, in houses of consequence, and may be manufactured in satin-wood, rose-wood, mahogany, or India woods; the decorative parts executed in *or molu* or bronzed metal, in opposition to the other materials used; the lower part in these articles, when inclosed as Plate 123, is fitted up with drawers to contain coins or other articles of curiosity; the front of the upper part is hinged at the base, and falls forward, making when down a desk for writing, &c.; the inside is fitted up in part with small drawers, and in part with pigeon-holes; the frieze in each of these Designs forms a drawer, opened and secured by a private spring and catch. In Plate 124 the plinth at bottom, as also the block on the top, are supposed to be of black marble.

PLATES 125 B, 126 C, and 127.—*Cheval Dressing Glasses.*

The three Designs in these Plates are supposed to be manufactured of mahogany, although frequently made of satin or rose wood, and not unfrequently executed to imitate bronzed metal, the ornaments being then gilt; they should be made to move on casters concealed in the feet or plinths; the ornaments on the standards and round the frame of the Glass in Plate 127 are meant as an inlay of ebony or brass.

PLATE 128.—*Bason Stands.*

The three Designs on this Plate admit of the same variety in woods for their manufacture as the three preceding Plates; the first and third Designs have a drawer in the plinth over the chimera feet; the top, containing the bason, is of statuary or grey marble, let in and made level with the top molding. The centre Design has its bason concealed by the ornamental frieze: supposing this to be stationary in the room where placed, the bason may be supplied with water by a pipe carried up the centre of the stem, and the water again carried off by a pipe with a plug at the bottom ot the bason, concealed also in the stem.

PLATE 129.—*Night Tables.*

In both these Designs the bottom part draws out as is usual in such pieces of furniture; in the first figure the pannel under the top is hinged at bottom, and falls down as in escrotoires, being released by a spring catch behind the lion's head; the doors in the second Design are hinged, and open as usual; the top and shelves are of marble, a plate of glass being placed at the back of the upper one; the chimeras supporting the middle shelf may be executed in wood, bronzed or gilt, or made in metal.

PLATE 130.—*Pot Cupboards.*

These ornamental articles are calculated for dressed Chambers, to be placed on each side the bed; the upper shelf serving for china, either for ornament or use, and forming at the same time a Table useful in case of indisposition. Casters may be concealed in the plinths or feet, making them moveable at pleasure. The ornaments in these Designs are intended to be carved in wood, and bronzed in imitation of metal.

PLATE 131.—*Double Chest of Drawers.*

An article of such general use does not stand in need of description. This Design is made lower than is usual, to avoid the disagreeable alternative of getting on chairs to place any thing in the upper drawers; for common use, no wood can be more serviceable than mahogany; for ornament, rose-wood with brass inlay, or satin-wood with black, may however be adopted. This piece of furniture might also be placed on casters, a matter never attended to, though certainly with its advantages, where cleanliness is attended to.

PLATES 132, 133, 134.—*Wardrobes.*

These very useful appendages to the dressing room and bed chamber are made single or with wings: in the former, the lower part contains drawers, three or five at pleasure; the upper part is filled with sliding shelves for clothes: in the latter, the wings are usually calculated to hold dresses, to be suspended on arms sliding on an iron rod. In Plate 132 the drawers are concealed in the lower carcase by folding doors, and the same in Plate 133. In Plate 134 drawers are intended to be made in the plinth supporting the whole, as well as in the upper panels of the wings under the carved ornamental cornice. The decoration in the Designs 132 and 134 may be carved and bronzed, or executed wholly in mahogany; the ornaments on Plate 133 are supposed as inlaid with ebony.

PLATES 135 A, and 136 B.—*Mirrors.*

In apartments where an extensive view offers itself, these Glasses become an elegant and useful ornament, reflecting objects in beautiful perspective on their convex surfaces; the frames, at the same time they form an elegant decoration on the walls, are calculated to support lights. In Plate 135 the vases on each side are intended for this purpose. In Plate 136 Sconces are put as usual; profiles of the moldings for the circles are added to each Design, which should be bold; in general, they will admit of being executed in bronze and gold, but will be far more elegant if executed wholly in gold.

PLATE 137.—*Chandelier.*

This Design is intended to be manufactured for the chief part in wood, the eagle carrying it being suspended in the centre of the ceiling of the apartment where used. As in Mirrors, this article of decoration may be executed as shewn in bronze and gold, or wholly gilt. The dimension must be regulated by the size of the room such article is intended for, the lowermost part placed at least seven feet from the ground. These Chandeliers will admit of twenty-four lights if required.

PLATE 138.—*Girandole.*

Different only in the mode of fixing from the preceding article; the use is the same; in rooms of considerable length, where a single Chandelier would not afford sufficient light, Girandoles are fixed at the extremities of apartments in pannels against the wall; they are equally serviceable in apartments where Chandeliers are not used. The manner of finishing them, either in bronze or gold, will be the same as those of the preceding Plates.

PLATE 139.—*Candelabra and Pedestal.*

These supports for Lights are placed in the angles of drawing rooms, and are used alternately for this purpose, as well as to carry transparent alabaster or glass vases. In apartments of state, where the furniture is made stationary, these Pedestals may be placed by the sides of large sofas, in continuation throughout the length of the room.

PLATE 140.—*Chandelier.*

What has been said on Plate 137 may be applied to the present subject, the use and manner of finishing it falling under the same regulation.

PLATE 141.—*Girandole, Vases, and Candlesticks.*

The particular Description of Plate 138 will answer for the Girandole in this: the Candlesticks and Vases are intended for chimney mantles, and should be executed in chased metal, imitating *or molu.*

PLATE 142.—*Pedestals for Statues, Busts, &c.*

In galleries for pictures or antiquities these Supports are appropriate for Busts or Statues; they are equally useful in halls and on staircases, and need not be rejected in drawing rooms, if executed in wood carved and gilt, in which case they answer conveniently to support vases of flowers, or figures carrying branches for lights. The Designs in the present Plate are supposed to be manufactured in wood, painted in imitation of antique marble.

PLATES 143 and 144.—*Jardiniers, Flower Stands, &c.*

These articles are appendages to drawing rooms, boudoirs, &c. and may be executed with every variety of taste and elegance agreeable to the rooms they are intended for; in mahogany they may be partly gilt or bronzed, in rose-wood part gold only; or they may be wholly gilt or japanned, as Plate 144, which Design is very well adapted for the ends of a long gallery or staircase, or to fill the space of a wide Venetian window, whether in a room or on the landing of an elegant staircase.

PLATES 145 A, 146 B.—*Decoration.*

These Plates are given as specimens of Designs, useful to the paper-hanger and decorator; the Egyptian style is chosen in the first, and in Plate 146 is given a specimen of decoration after the Etruscan, compiled from specimens discovered at Herculaneum. These two pannels are appropriate for the ends of rooms, or the spaces on each side a chimney. In Plate 145 the cornice of the room should be finished in oil gold, the fringe painted a mazarine blue, the stars of composition, projecting and finished in clean matt gold. The dado of apartments thus finished should be painted to imitate antique marble.

PLATES 147 C, and 148 D.—*Chimney Glass and Decoration.*

These Plates represent part of the longest sides of an apartment, where the chimnies are usually placed, the arrangement and Decoration of which is now given, shewing likewise the mode in which the Looking-glass as also the frames are proportioned in respect to the chimney piece. The Decoration of the frame in Plate 147 is meant to be carved in wood,

E 2

and finished to imitate bronzed metal; the vases on the mantle-piece are intended to be real metal, part bronzed and part *or molu*; the ornaments on the chimney-piece must be of metal gilt or pale lacquered, where the expense is considered; the Decoration on the walls are on paper, and painted by hand. In Plate 148 the rustic frame is wood, carved and bronzed, the ornament at the top with its side ornaments are painted on the wall, with the other Decorations of the room; the vases suspended from the frame are intended to carry lights, and may also be executed in wood and gilt; the vases on the mantle-piece are supposed to be real Etruscan.

PLATE 149.—*Design for a Drawing Room in the Chinese Taste.*

This Design for an elegant Drawing Room comprehends the long side, containing the chimney-piece, which is made to represent a Chinese Temple: a large plate of glass fits exactly the space between the decorative pilasters of the room, against which Chinese Plants and Trees are fixed, carved in wood: a glass of similar dimensions and style being fixed on the opposite side of the room would produce a most pleasing effect from double reflection. As nothing contributes more to a real good effect than actual shadow produced by projection, the space on each side the chimney is made to recede, thus admitting of real architectural decoration, as Columns, &c. which are after the Chinese taste. These Columns may be covered with *scagliola,* or imitation of marble; the bases and capitals, as likewise the Decorations, are of gold: the opposite side of the room being in correspondence, will admit of twelve lamps for lights, in addition to the central chandelier, which may be uniformly suspended from brackets. In each recess should be an Ottoman.

The walls in this apartment should be painted to answer in every particular the window side, giving a Chinese landscape in the parts allotted to the windows, over which should be represented the Chinese blind or curtain when rolled up. The good effect of this Design will depend much on the taste of the parties superintending its execution, who should be well versed in the Chinese style, and avoid introducing any species of ornament and arrangement not in accordance with this peculiar taste, which has been often improperly used in rooms too small and insignificant for any decoration to produce an imposing effect on the spectator. A room like this, set apart as a drawing-room, should be hung with rich one-coloured satin or velvet, the Chinese papers being better calculated for plain or secondary apartments: where expense is not spared and magnificence is required, a border might be worked in embroidery to surround each pannel: the carpets would answer best if made of the Wilton manufacture and of one colour, surrounded with a rich Chinese border, kept two feet from the wall.

PLATE 150.—*Drawing Room Decoration in the Gothic Style.*

This example has been composed under the same arrangement as the preceding Design, the only difference being in the style, which admits of more variety in point of finishing: for example, the walls of this room may be hung with satin or velvet, and covered with Gothic tracery work, carved and richly gilt; or the Gothic work might be executed in oak, the hollows being gilt, the wall or grounds picked-in a rich crimson colour. A rich candelabra might be placed with great propriety before each pier, joining the recesses. Great care should be taken in fitting up apartments after this fashion to adopt an uniformity of ornament, and not to introduce any melange of dates and styles. The florid Gothic has been chosen in this Design from its light effect, in preference to earlier examples, which, however much bordering on the Grecian style, are too massive for interior Decoration.

PLATE 151.—*Boudoir with Ottomans.*

In this Design the whole decoration is after the antique. The mantles on the walls are meant to be real, and of satin, muslin, or superfine cassimere; the borders worked in needlework or printed; the staffs supporting the drapery are finished in matt gold.   Ottomans occupy the four sides of the room ; the openings, as doors and windows, having Chimeras on each side, executed in imitation of gold and bronze.   The whole of this ornamental Design may be executed in water-colour, on the walls, by a skilful artist, with good effect.   The floor should be covered with Wilton carpeting of a plain colour.

PLATES 152 and 153.—*State Drawing Room, shewing its Decoration and Furniture, with a Section and Plan of the same.*

These Plates shew how essential architecture is towards producing grandeur of effect in an apartment of elegance and consequence, without which, although beauty may be obtained, a grand style never can be produced.   The business of Decoration being generally entrusted to the vender of paper-hangings, it is perhaps too much to expect any thing like arrangement or rule : the same happens repeatedly where the Decoration is entrusted to artists, who, although capable of producing good effects by the pencil, are totally unacquainted with any architectural rules by which to govern their proportions.   A knowledge, therefore, of architecture, so far as relates to the general proportions of the Orders, as it gives a facility in making and arranging plans in proportion, becomes indispensable to the Upholder as well as to the Architect.   The knowledge of this science once obtained will produce a taste for uniformity ; and its rules, which are the groundwork of so much method and precision, cannot fail of producing a pleasing effect in the performances of those who devote a portion of their time to its study.

Of the present Design, the columns afford recesses, and give space for the reception of the Sofas, and thereby prevent them projecting into the room ; a recess is made also between the pilasters, opposite the chimney, in which is placed a marble Table, supported on Chimeras carved and gilt ; a subplinth is given to the columns and pilasters, equal to the height of the Chairs and Sofas, by which means the view of the architecture is preserved entire. In rooms of large dimensions, a Table placed in the centre may be stationary, round which should be placed four Chaises Longue, and at each angle a Candelabra to support candles or lamps. The Chairs placed in this room are also supposed to be stationary, lighter ones being dispersed about the room for use.

A Drawing Room of such consequence should be hung with damask or velvet; the shafts of the columns and parts of the architecture, supposed to be statuary marble, may be finished in white, highly polished; the capitals and bases of the columns carved and finished in gold; the ornaments in the pilasters and frieze, as well as the moldings of the cornice, &c. all in the same style. For the windows, the Curtains should be crimson, to suit the walls; the Draperies blue, having a gold fringe to both: the opposite side to the windows being similar in its plan and arrangement, must have Draperies and Curtains attached to the walls behind the Sofas. The Glass over the chimney, is secured by the pilasters, and needs no other frame. The middle recess on this side of the Room, as shewn in the Section, is made into a window, having the Glass of one entire plate, without any sash bars: a plate of looking-glass slides within the wall, which at night is to be drawn over the window; the Drapery round which is made *en suite* with the side windows. The ceiling being painted as a sky, any Chandelier suspended from it has been avoided; instead of which, four smaller lights are hung from the soffit at the termination of the cove.

In Plate 153 a plan is given, which shews the arrangement of the Chairs, Sofas, &c. in which Candelabri are placed in the angles of the room. In the geometrical elevation of the side of this apartment, the Chandeliers suspended from the cove are omitted, as they would have greatly confused the pilasters, and their effect is clearly shewn in the perspective view. On the same account the Candelabri in the angles of the Room have been omitted, their places being shewn in the Plan. The Carpet for this State Apartment should be of a plain colour in the middle, and of Wilton or Axminster manufacture: a rich border in gold-colour might be worked round it, to answer the cove, and set two feet from the wall, to be clear from the furniture.

Such a Room should not open immediately to the staircase; a circular or octangular vestibule is necessary, which should be fitted up equally well in its decorations, though plainer. At the opposite end should be a Withdrawing Room, opening likewise on a staircase, thus admitting the Company one way, and allowing their departure by another; all which is easily arranged in houses built expressly for persons of fashion, and by which the confusion attendant on large assemblies may be greatly avoided.

PLATES 154 and 155.—*Moldings for Glass Frames, &c.*

The first of these Plates contains Designs for Picture and Glass Frame Moldings, with the whole of their decoration, and profiles attached to each. For Pictures, all mixture should be avoided, the Frames executed solely in gold; for Glass Frames, a mixture of bronze may be admitted. In Plate 155, the arrangement is given for the mitre angles, on which are placed blocks admitting over them an ornamental termination. Profiles are given for the respective Moldings of these Frames, affording sufficient explanation to the workman.

PLATES 156 and 157.—*Profiles for Moldings for Cabinet Work.*

These Plates give an ample variety of Moldings for almost every sort of Cabinet Work, whether for cornices, filleting bands, or base moldings; at the same time they furnish sufficient examples to the Cabinet-maker for compilation. It will be needless to point out the kind of material they should be made of: it will ever be subject to circumstance and fancy. For general directions, the larger Moldings may be of mahogany, and the smaller in ebony or bronze: if the furniture be satin-wood, the larger members may follow the same arrangement.

PLATE 158.—*Fretts.*

This elegant ornament, of ancient invention, makes the happiest Design for borders, whether for our walls or floors ; it is equally beautiful in friezes, and admits of being used as much by the Carver as by the Weaver or Printer. Nothing can be more appropriate, applied in narrow pannels, placed at the top and bottom of doors, to break their too great length. The Japanner and Painter will find in this ornament an endless variety, which, under skilful hands, may be conducive in producing a better proportion in Designs, otherwise defective from their too great length or breadth.

THE END.

F

Printed by S. GOSNELL, Little Queen Street.

Plate 2.

Window Cornices and Drapery.

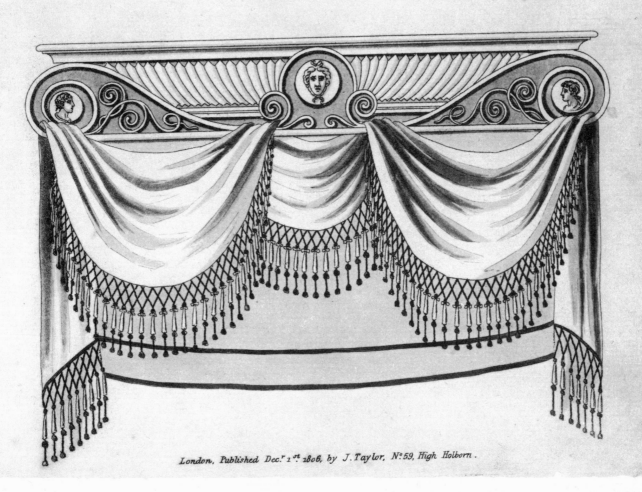

London, Published Dec.ʳ 1ˢᵗ 1806, by J. Taylor, Nº 59, High Holborn.

Plate 3.

Cornices and Drapery, in the Chinese style.

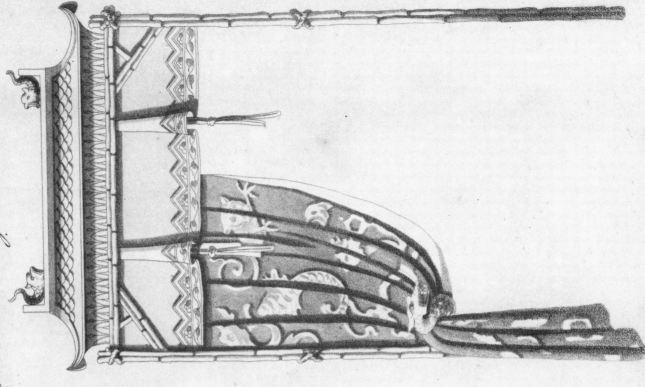

London. Published Dec.r 5.st 1806. by J. Taylor, 59. High Holborn.

A

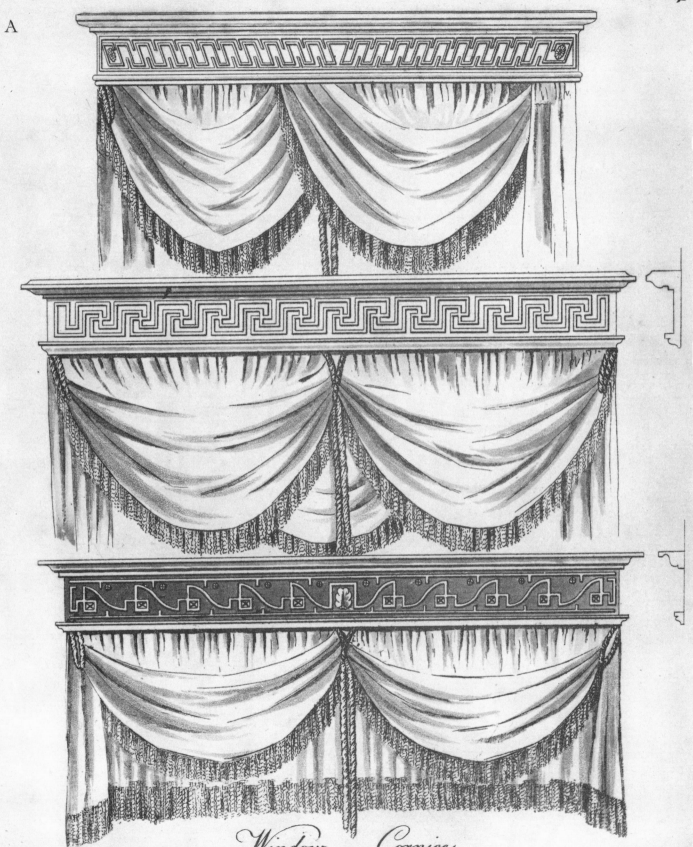

Window Cornices.

London. Published Dec.ʳ 1. 1804. by J. Taylor, Nᵒ 59 High Holborn.

Window Curtain.

London. Published July 1, 1805, by J. Taylor, No. 59, High Holborn.

London. Published Dec.ʳ 1. 1804, by J. Taylor, N.º 59 High Holborn.

Pl. 7.

Window Curtain.

London. Published July 1. 1805, by J. Taylor, N.º 59, High Holborn.

Pl. 8

A

Window Curtain.

London. Published Dec.ʳ 1. 1804, by J. Taylor, No 59 High Holborn.

Pl. 3

Military Window Curtain.

London. Published Dec.ʳ 1. 1804. by J. Taylon N.º 59 High Holborn.

Pl. 10.

A *Continued Drapery and Window Curtains* —

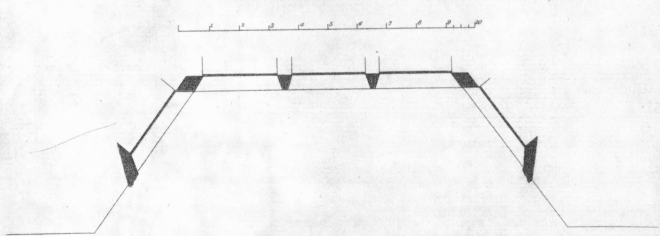

London Published July 1. 1805, by J. Taylor, N.º 59, High Holborn.

Pl. 11

Continued Drapery and Window Curtains.

B

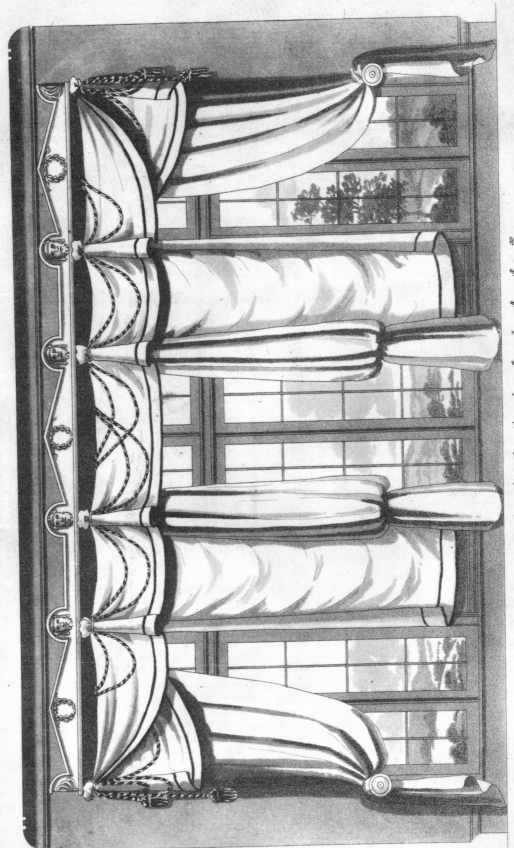

London Published July 1. 1805, by J.Taylor. Nº 59. High Holborn.

Plate 12.

Continued Drapery

London, Published Dec.ʳ 1ˢᵗ 1806. by J. Taylor, 59. High Holborn.

Plate 13.

Continued Drapery

London. Published. Dec.r 1.st 1806, by J.Taylor, 59, High Holborn.

Bed Pillars.

Plate 14.

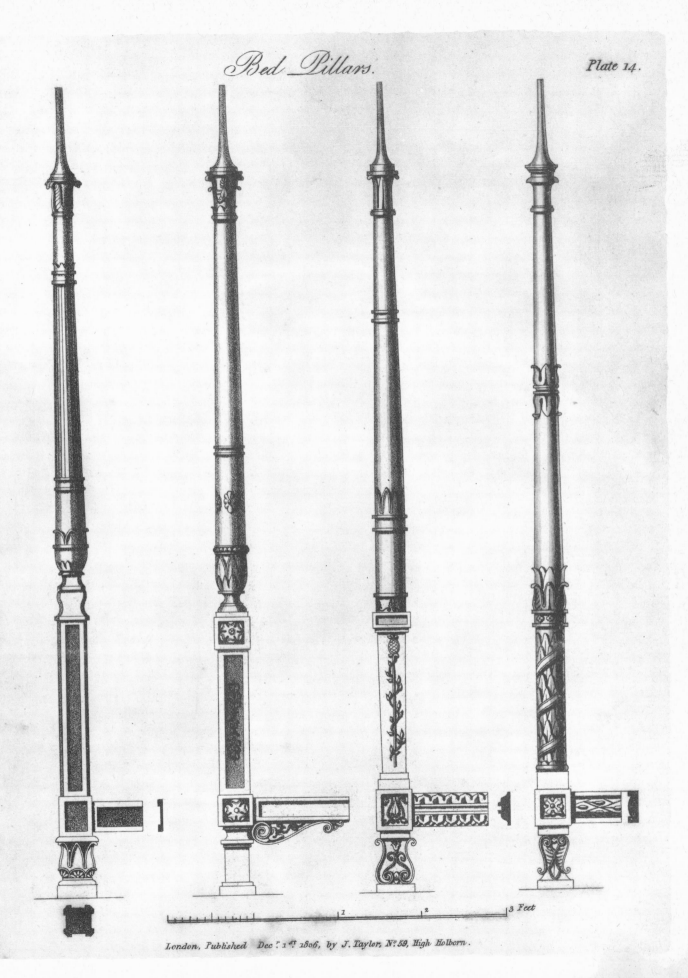

1   2   3 Feet

London, Published Dec.r 1.st 1806, by J. Taylor, N.o 59, High Holborn.

Pl. 15.

A

Bed Pillars with Foot-board.

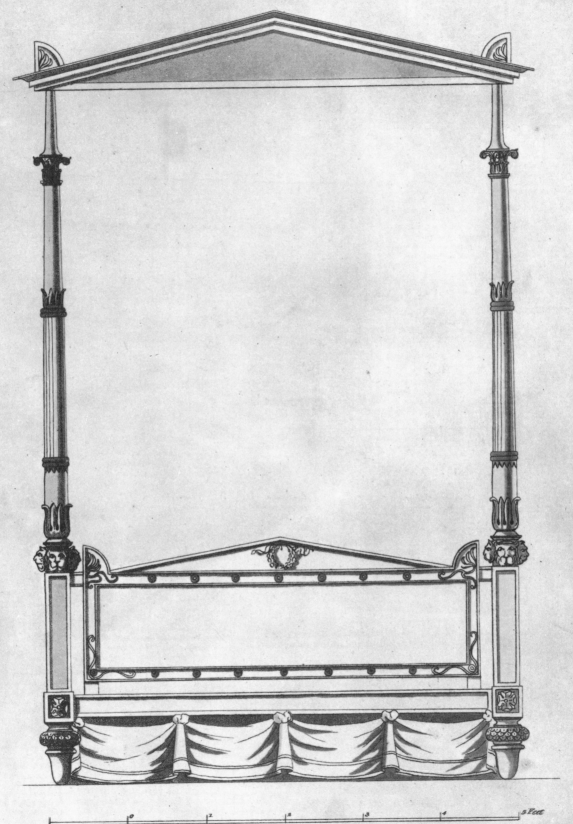

London. Published, July, 1.1805, by J.Taylor, N.º 59, High Holborn.

Pl. 16.

B

Bed Pillars with Foot-board.

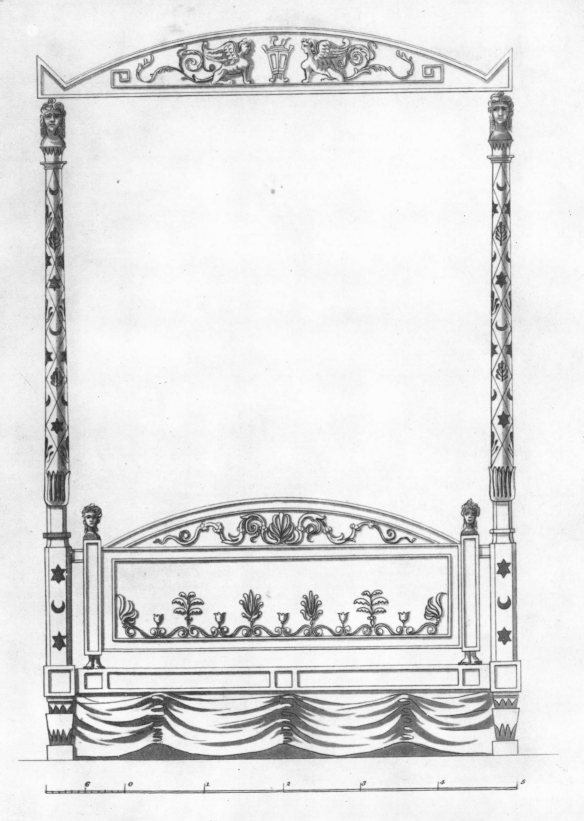

London. Published, July 1, 1805, by J. Taylor, N.º 59, High Holborn.

Bed Cornices.

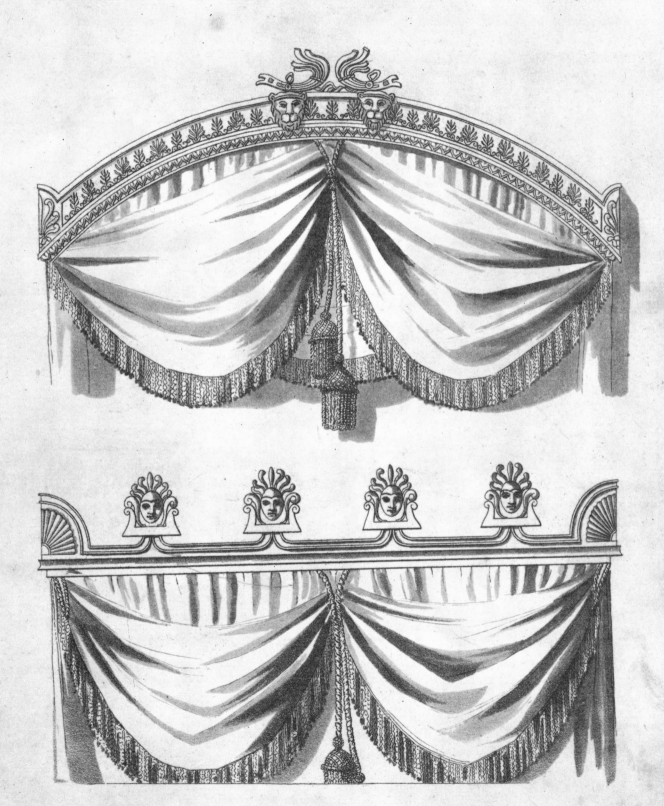

London. Published Dec.ʳ 1. 1804. by J. Taylor, N.º 59 High Holborn.

Plate 18.

Bed Cornices, in the Gothic style.

London, Published Dec.r 1.st 1806, by J. Taylor, 59, High Holborn.

Plate 19.

Cribb Bedstead.

London, Published Jan.ʳ 1ˢᵗ 1807, by J. Taylor, 59, High Holborn.

Plate 20.

Tent Bed.

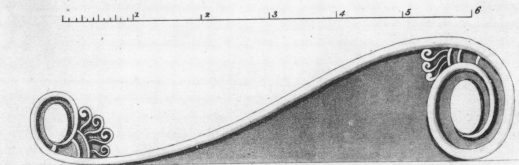

Profile of Teaster

London, Published Dec.r 1.st 1806, by J. Taylor, 59, High Holborn.

Plate 21.

Field Bed.

Profile of Bedstead

1   2   3   4   5 Feet

London, Published Dec.r 1st 1806, by J. Taylor, No. 59, High Holborn.

Pl. 22.

B

Design for a Bed.

London. Published, July, 1.1805, by J.Taylor, No.59, High Holborn.

Military Officers Bed.

Pl. 23

London. Published Dec.r 1.1804. by J. Taylor. N.o 59 High. Holborn.

Pl. 24

Design for a Dome Bed.

London. Published July 1.1805, by J.Taylor, Nº 59, High Holborn.

Pl. 25.

A

Design for a Bed.

London, Published July 1, 1805, by J. Taylor, No. 59, High Holborn.

Pl. 26

Design for a Bed.

London. Published. Dec.ᵗ 1.1804. by J. Taylor. N.º 59 High Holborn.

Pl. 27.

Polonaise Bed.

London Published July 1, 1805, by J. Taylor, N.º 59, High Holborn.

State Bed.

Plate 28.

London, Published Jan.1.st 1807, by J.Taylor. 59, High Holborn.

Pl 29.

French Bed.

London.Published July 1.1805, by J.Taylor, N.59, High Holborn.

Pl. 30

Pl. 30

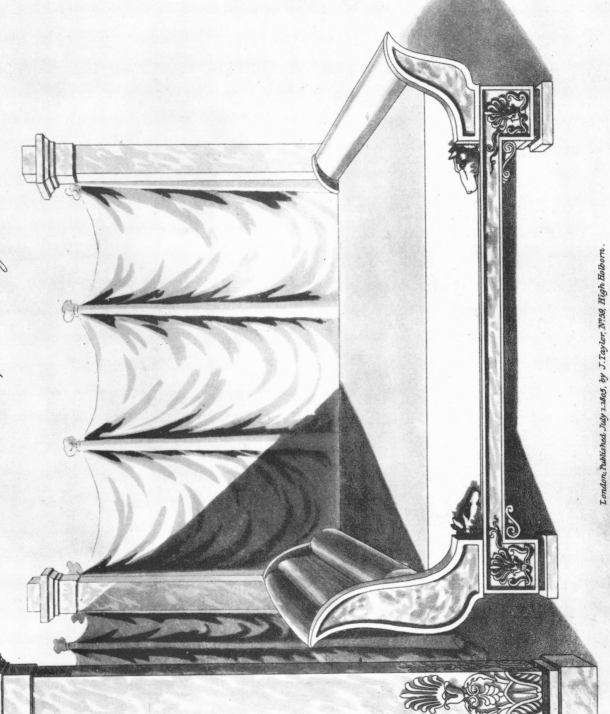

French Bed for a Recess.

London, Published July 1.1805, by J. Taylor, No. 59. High Holborn.

French Bed and Wardrobe.

Pl. 31

London, Published Dec.r 1, 1804 by J. Taylor N.o 59 High Holborn.

B

Pl. 32

French Bed and Wardrobe.

A

London. Published Dec.7.1804. by.I.Taylor, N.º.59 High Holborn.

Pl. 33.

Pl. 33

Bedsteps

London. Published July 1, 1805, by J. Taylor, No 59, High Holborn.

Pl. 34

Hall seats for Recesses.

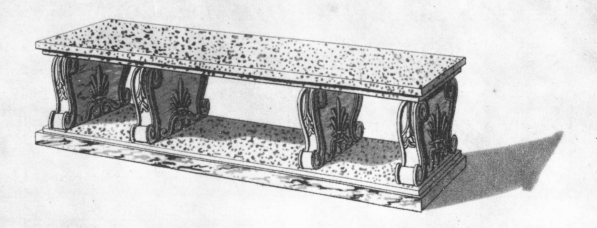

London, Published Dec.ʳ 1.1804, by J. Taylor, N.º 59 High Holborn.

Plate 35.

Hall Sofa.

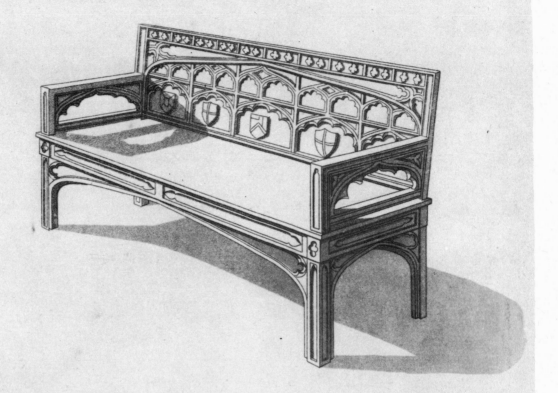

Hall Chairs.

London, Published Jan.¹ 1807. by J. Taylor. 59. High Holborn.

Plate 36.

Hall Chairs.

London, Published Jan.ʳ 2.ᵈ 1807, by J. Taylor, 59, High Holborn.

Parlor Chairs, fronts & profiles.

Plate 37.

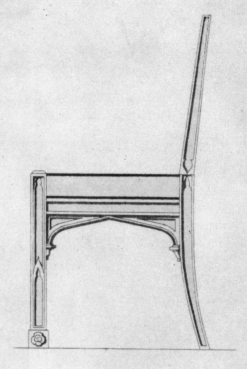

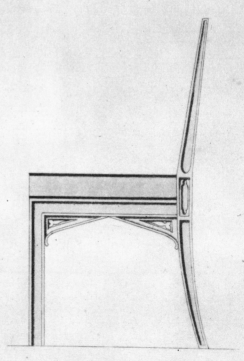

London, Published Jan.ᵗ 1.ˢᵗ 1807, by J.Taylor, 59, High Holborn.

Parlor Chairs fronts & profiles.

Plate 38.

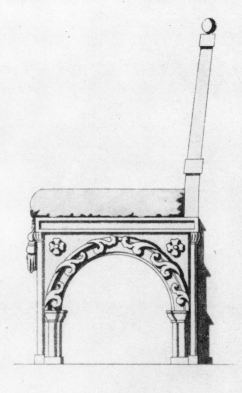

London, Published Jan.ʳ 1ˢᵗ 1807, by J. Taylor, 59, High Holborn.

Pl 39.

Pl 32

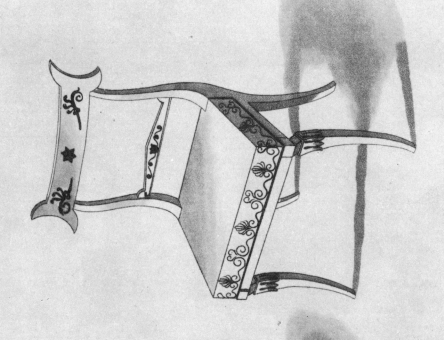

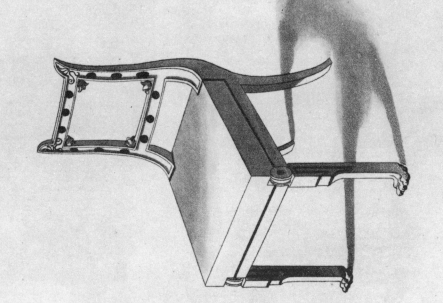

Parlor Chairs.

Seats — French Stuffed

London. Published July 1. 1805, by J.Taylor, Nº 59, High Holborn.

Pl 40.

Parlor Chairs.

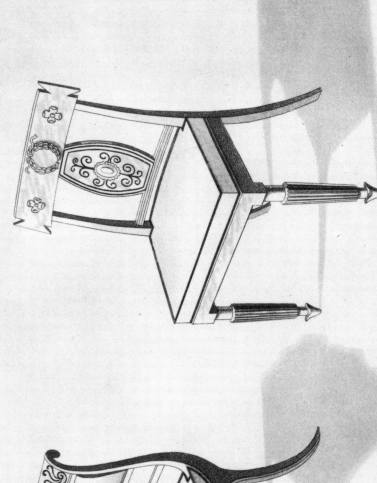

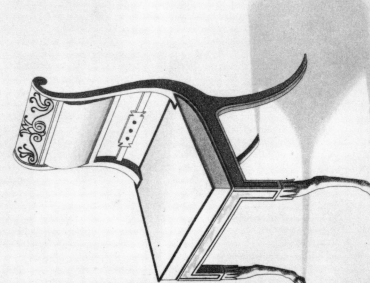

A

London. Published July 1.1805. by J.Taylor, Nᵒ59. High Holborn.

Pl.41.

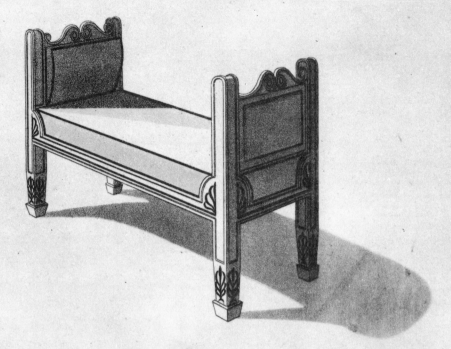

Library Seats

London. Published July 1.1805, by J.Taylor, N°.59, High Holborn .

Plate 42.

Library Fauteuil
with Desk and Sliding Footstool.

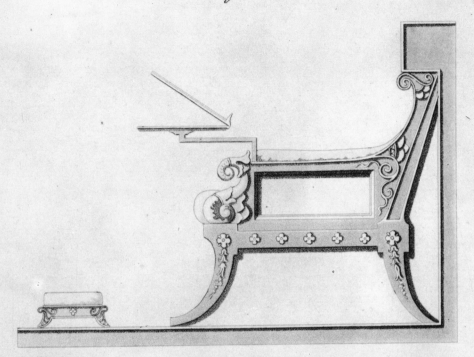

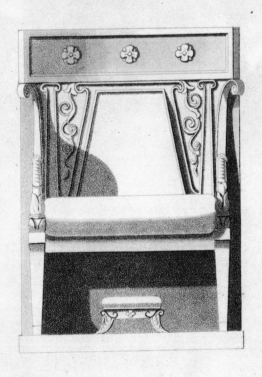

London, Published Jan'.1''. 1807, by J.Taylor, 59, High Holborn .

Pl. 51

Tête a Tête Seats.

London Published Dec.r 1.1804. by J.Taylor, N.o 59 High Holborn.

Pl. 52

Window Seats.

London, Published Dec.ᵗ 1, 1804, by J. Taylor, Nº 59 High Holborn.

Plate 53.

Drawing Room X Seats.

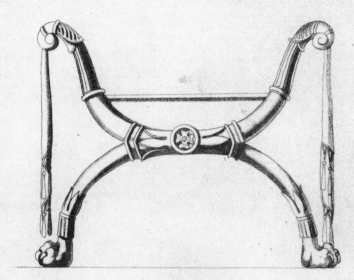

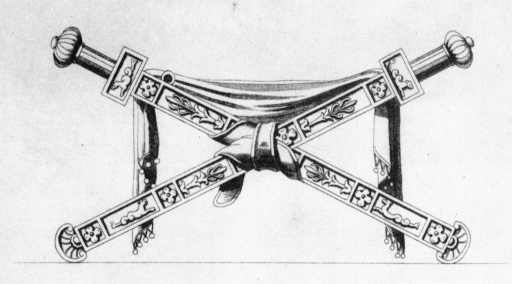

London. Published Jan.1.1807. by J.Taylor. 59. High Holborn.

Plate 54.

Drawing Room Chairs, in Profile.

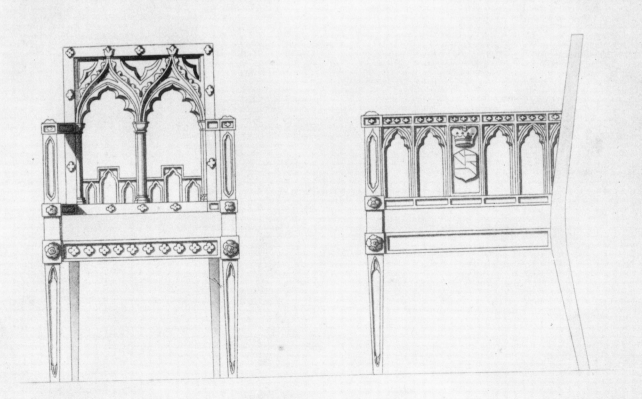

London, Published Jan.ʳ 1ˢᵗ 1807, by J.Taylor, 59, High Holborn .

Pl. 55.

Drawing Room Chairs in Profile.

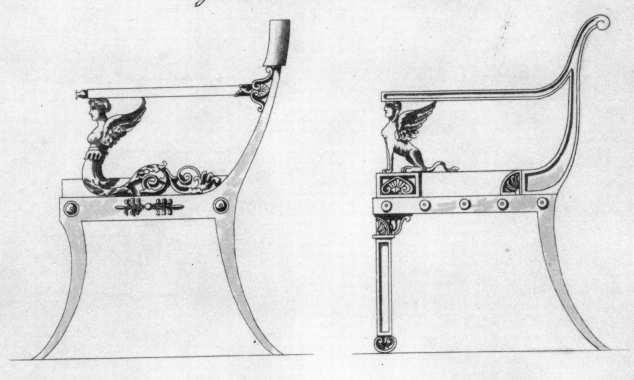

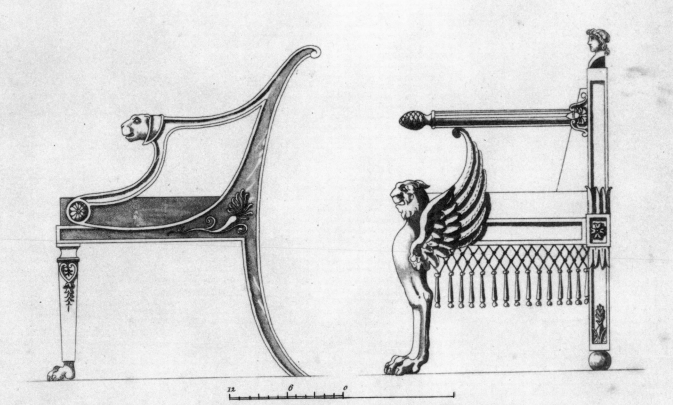

12   6   0

London, Published July 1. 1805, by J. Taylor, No. 59, High Holborn.

Pl 56

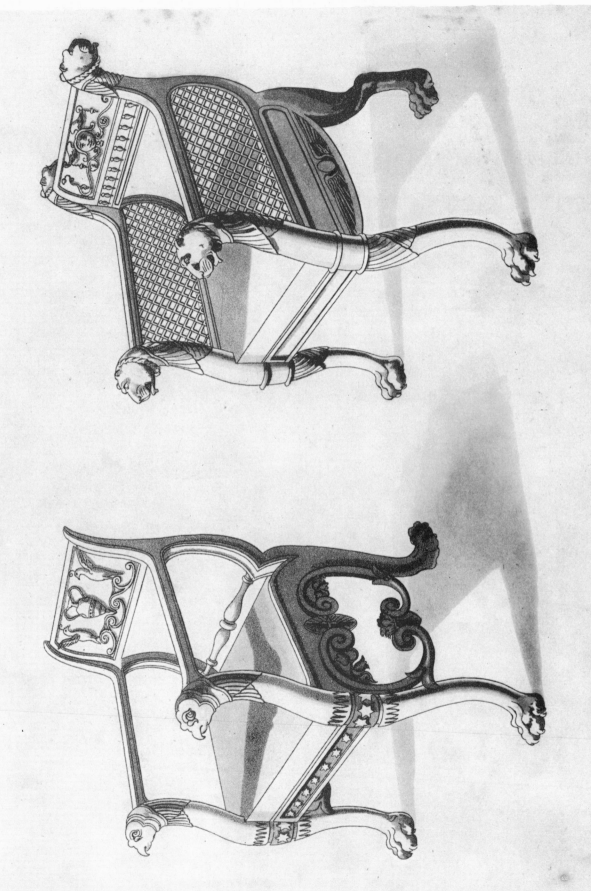

Drawing room Chairs

London. Published Dec.r 1. 1804, by J.Taylor, N.o 59 High Holborn.

C

Plate 57.

Drawing Room Chairs and Backs.

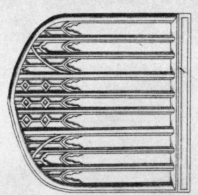

London, Published Jan'y. 1st. 1807, by J. Taylor, 59, High Holborn.

Plate 58.

Drawing Room State Chair.

London, Published Jan.ʸ 1.ˢᵗ 1807, by J. Taylor, 59, High Holborn.

Pl 59

Sofas.

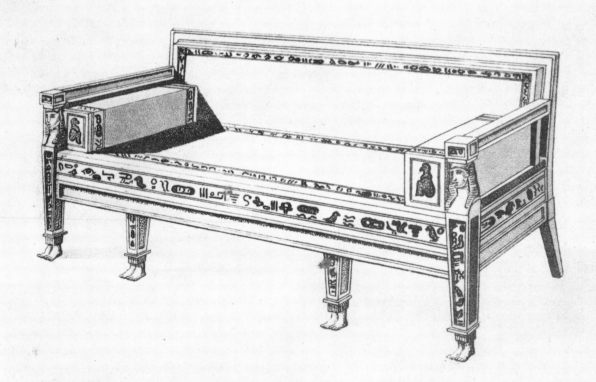

London. Published Dec.ʳ 1. 1804 by J. Taylor N.º 59 High Holborn .

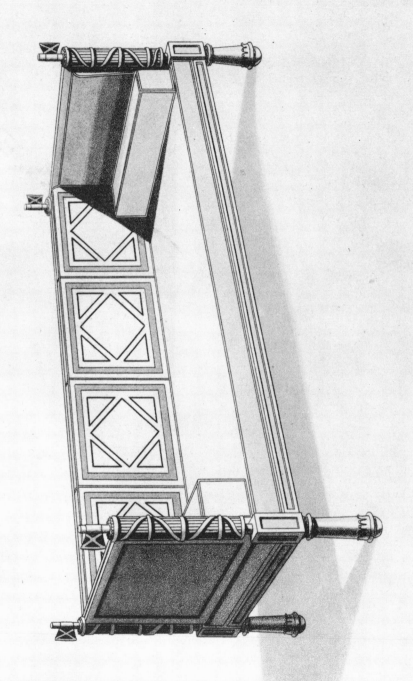

Library Sofa.

London. Published. July 1 1805. by J.Taylor. Nᵒ 59 High. Holborn.

Plate 61.

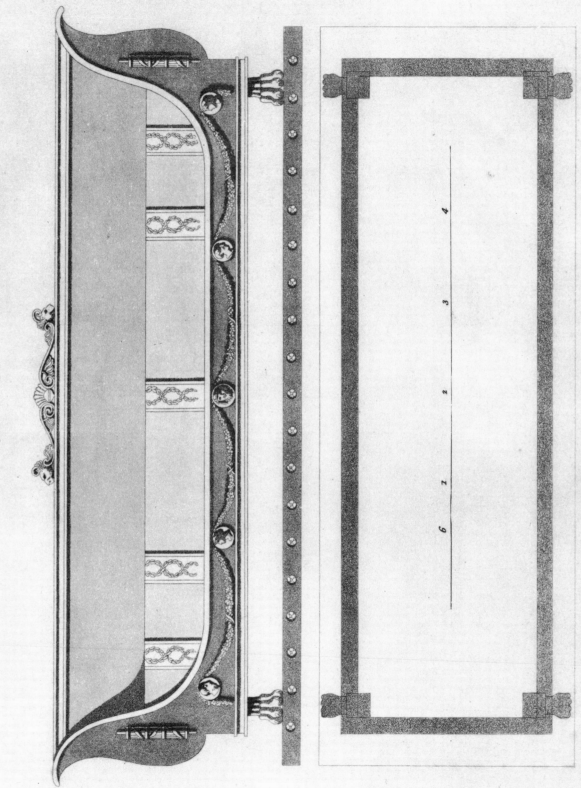

Drawing Room Sofa.

A

London, Published Dec.r 1.st 1806. by J. Taylor, 59. High Holborn.

Plate 62.

Drawing Room Sofa.

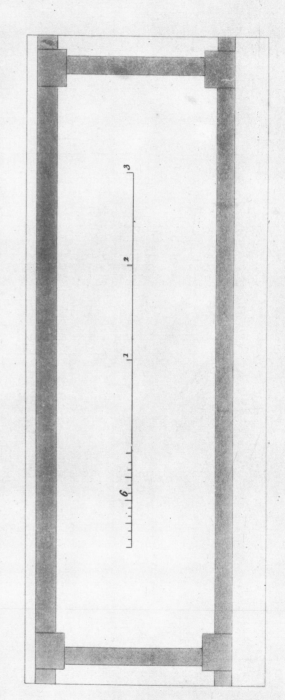

London, Published Dec.ʳ 1.ˢᵗ 1806, by J.Taylor, 59, High Holborn.

B

Plate 63.

Chaise Longue in Profile.

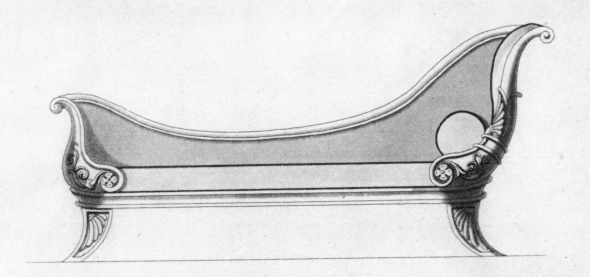

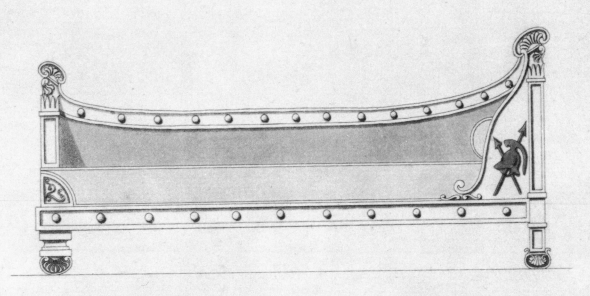

London, Published Dec.r 1.st 1806, by J.Taylor, 59, High Holborn.

Pl. 64.

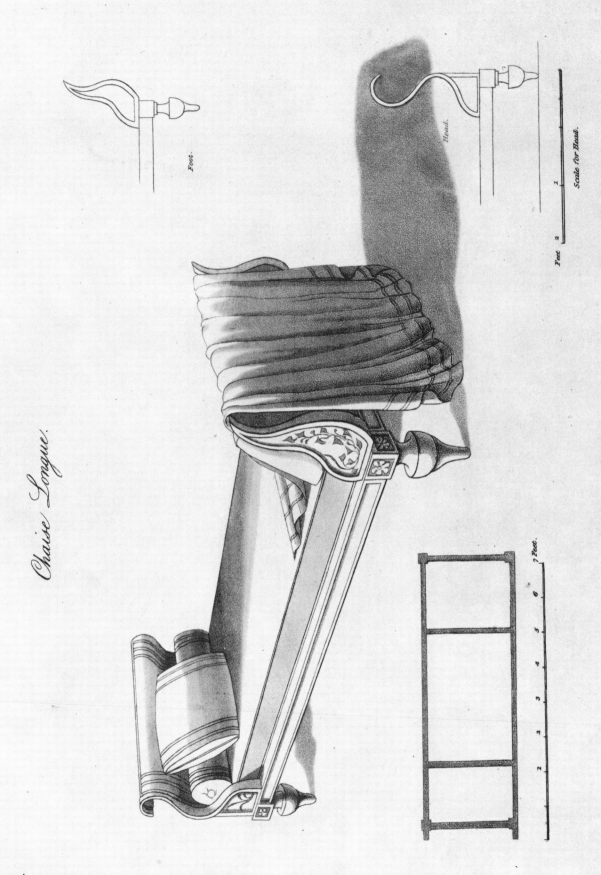

Chaise Longue.

Foot.

Head.

Scale for Head.

Feet 2   1

7 Feet.

A

London. Published July, 1. 1805, by J. Taylor, Nº 59, High Holborn.

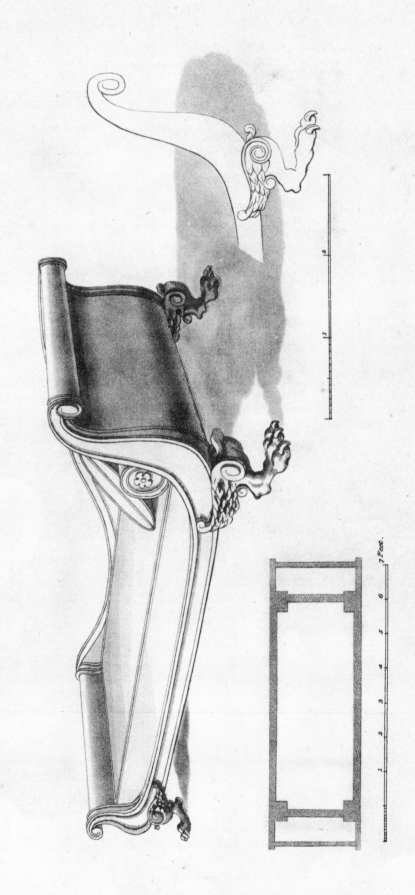

Chaise Longue.

London.Published July 1.1805 by J.Taylor, N.º59 High Holborn.

Pl. 66

Chaise Longue.

London. Published. Dec.ᵗʰ 7.1804, by J. Taylor, Nº.59 High Holborn.

Plate 67.

Ottoman for Gallery

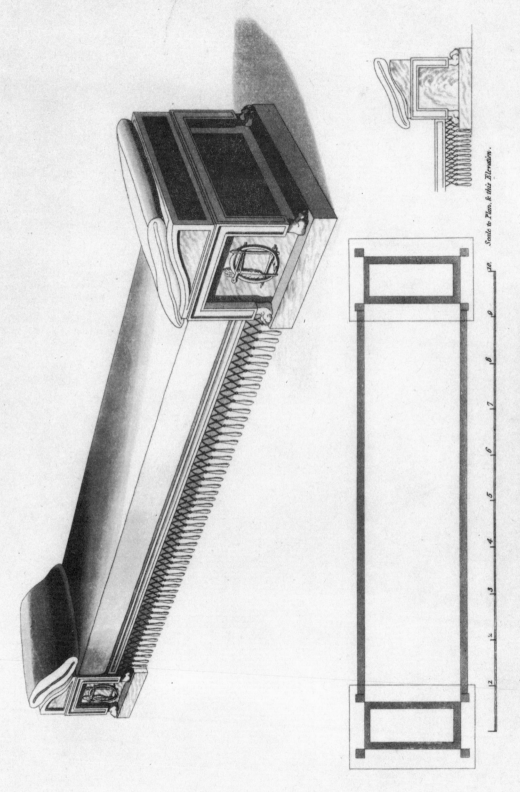

Scale to Plan & this Elevation.

London, Published Dec.r 1.st 1806, by J. Taylor, 59 High Holborn.

Plate 68.

Ottoman for Music Room.

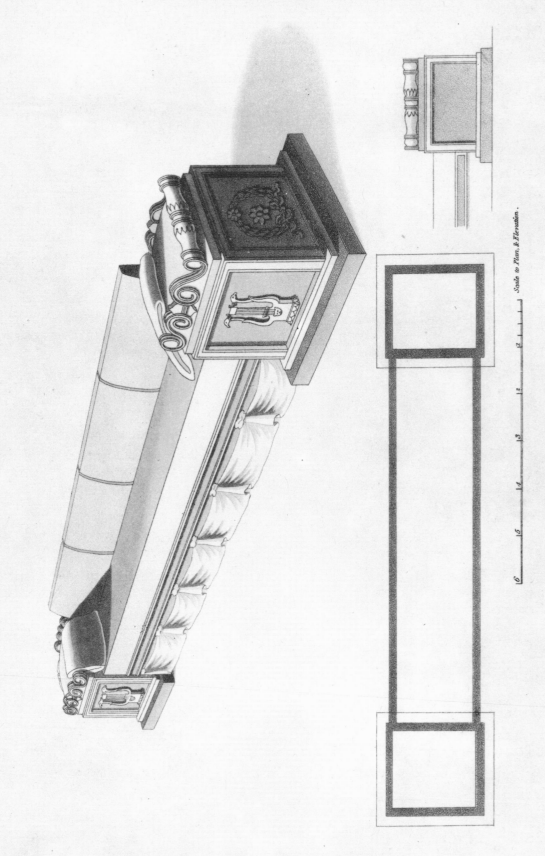

London, Published Dec 5.ᵗ 1806, by J.Taylor, 59, High Holborn.

Scale to Plan, & Elevation.

Pillar and Claw Table.

Plate 69.

Fig. 1.

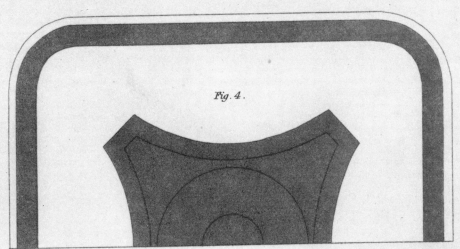

Fig. 4.

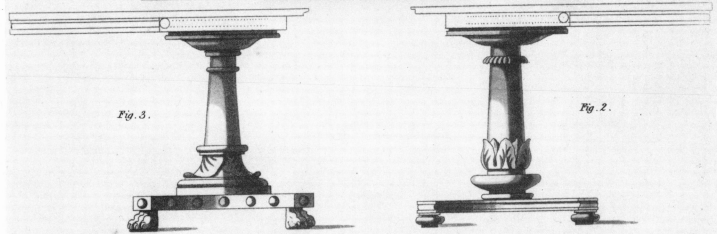

Fig. 3.

Fig. 2.

London, Published Jan.ᵗ 1ˢᵗ 1807, by J. Taylor, 59, High Holborn.

Plate 70.

Harlequin Table.

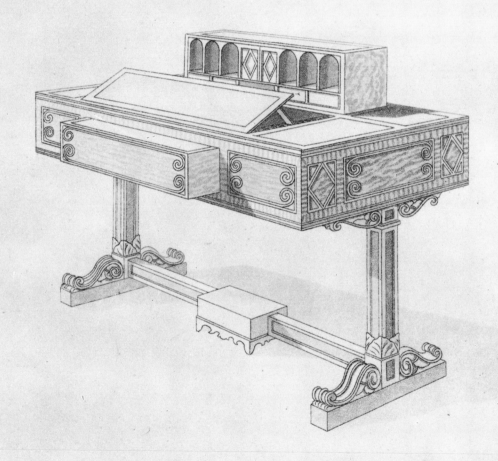

London, Published Jan'y 1st 1807, by J. Taylor, 59, High Holborn.

Plate 71.

Gentleman's Dressing Table.

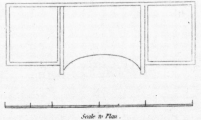

Scale to Plan.

London, Published Jan.ʳ 1.ˢᵗ 1807, by J. Taylor, 59, High Holborn.

Pl 72.

Dressing Tables.

London, Published July 1. 1805, by J. Taylor, Nº 59, High Holborn.

Plate 73.

Ladies Dressing Table.

4 *Scale to Plan.*

London, Published Dec 1.st 1806, by J. Taylor, No 59, High Holborn.

Plate 74.

Ladies Dressing Table and Glass.

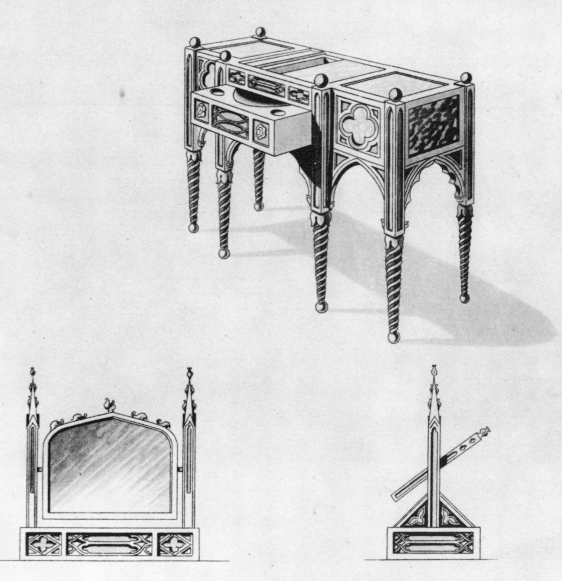

London, Published Jan.ʸ 1ˢᵗ 1807, by J. Taylor, 59, High Holborn.

Pl.75.

Work Table.

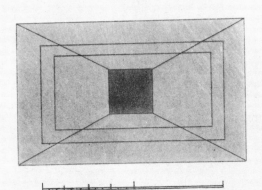

London. Published July 1. 1805, by J Taylor, N.º 59, High Holborn.

Pl. 76.

Work Tables.

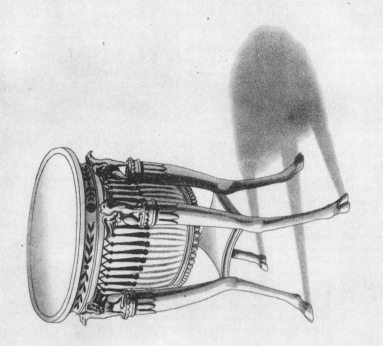

London. Published, July, 1.1805, by J.Taylor, Nº59.High Holborn .

Pl 77

Work Tables

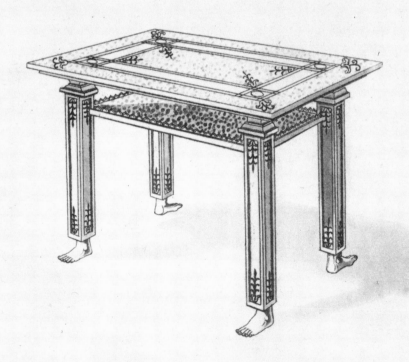

London. Publish'd Dec.1. 1804, by J.Taylor, N.º59 High Holborn.

Plate 78.

Backgammon Work Table

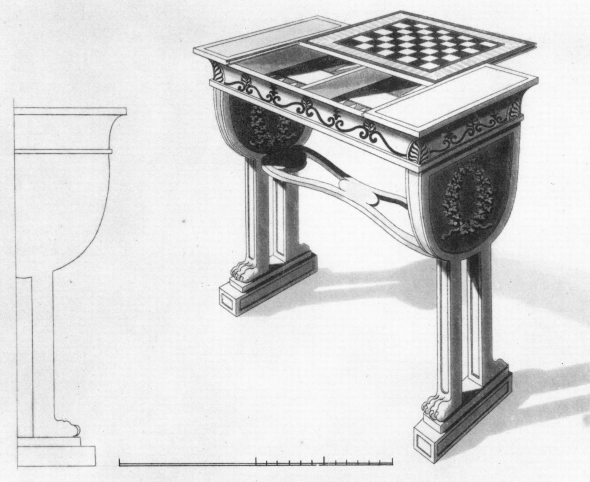

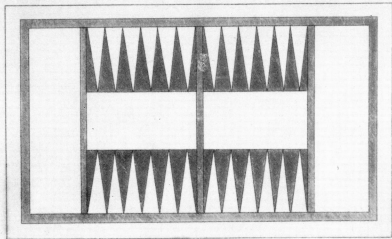

London, Published Dec.r 1.st 1806, by J. Taylor, 59, High Holborn.

Plate 79.

Tea Poys.

Quartetto Tables.

Canterburys.

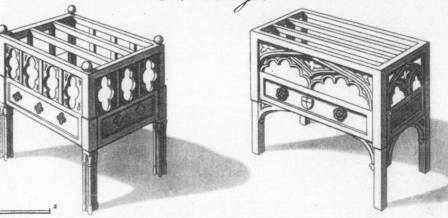

London, Published Jan.¹ 1ˢᵗ 1807, by J. Taylor, 59, High Holborn.

Plate 30.

Screen Writing & Work Table.

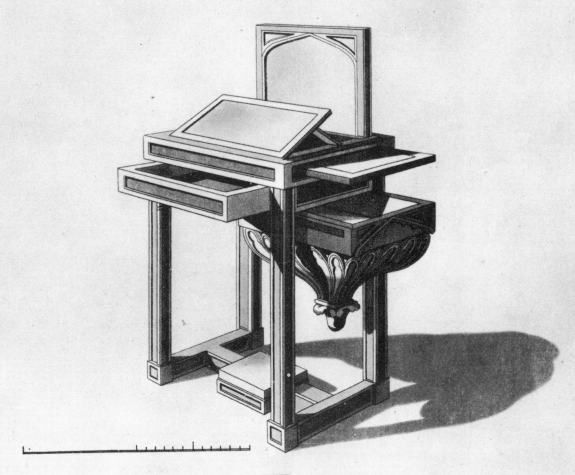

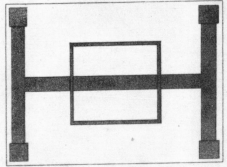

London, Published Jan.ᵗ 1.st 1807, by J.Taylor, 59, High Holborn.

Plate 81.

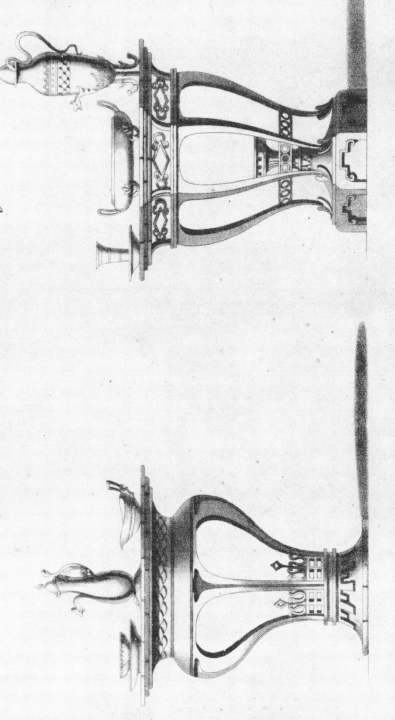

Dejune Tables, in the Chinese style.

London, Published Dec.r 1.st 1806 by J.Taylor 59 High Holborn.

Pl. 82.

Dejuné Table.

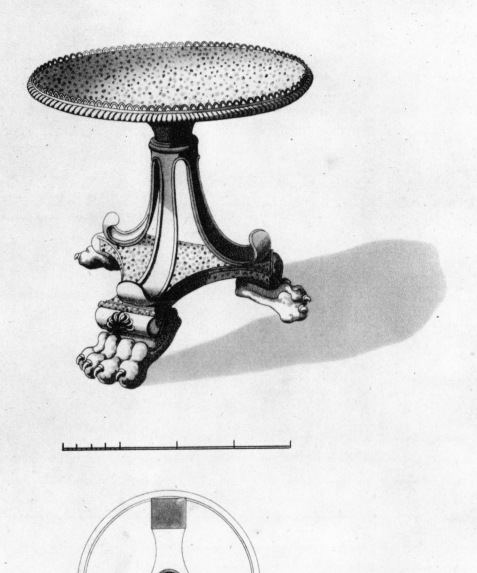

London. Published July 1. 1805, by J. Taylor, No. 59, High Holborn.

Sofa Table.

Pl. 83

A

London. Published, Dec.r 1. 1804, by J. Taylor, Nº 59, High Holborn.

Sofa Table.

Pl 84

London. Published Dec.r 1. 1804, by J. Taylor, N.º 59, High Holborn.

Plate 85.

Sofa Table.

Scale to Plan.

1   2   3   4   5   6

Footstool

Scale to Profile & Footstool.

1   2   3

London, Published Jan.'1.st 1807, by J. Taylor, 59, High Holborn.

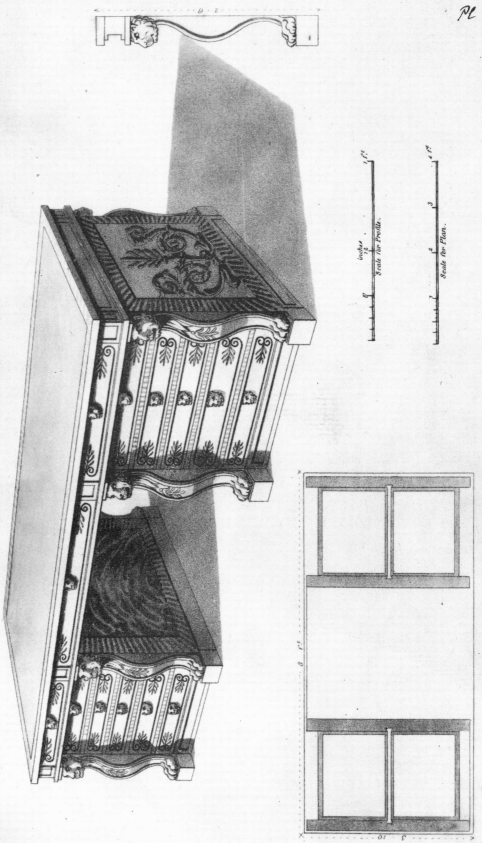

Library Table.

Pl 86

inches

Scale for Profile.

Scale for Plan.

London. Published Dec.1. 1804, by J.Taylor, N.°59 High Holborn.

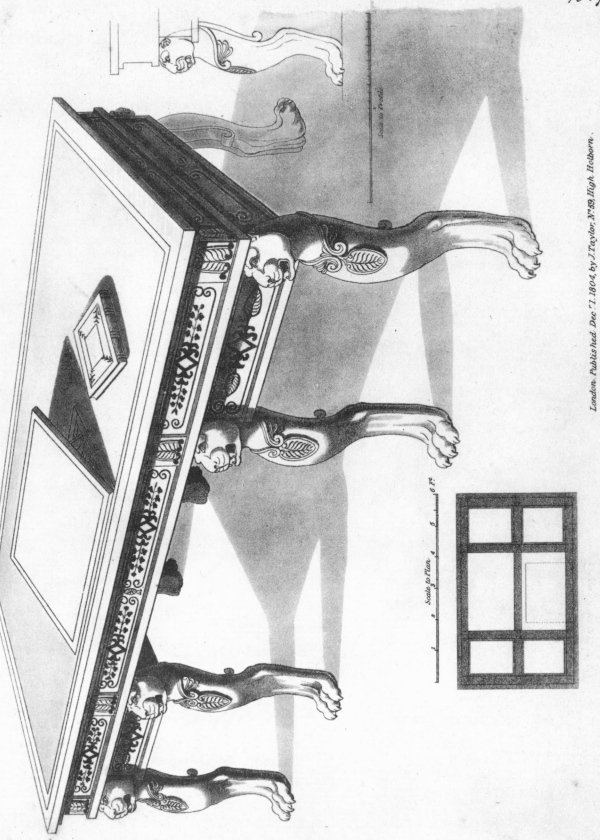

Library Table

London. Published Dec.r 1. 1804, by J. Taylor, No 59, High Holborn.

Scale to Plan.

Pl 87

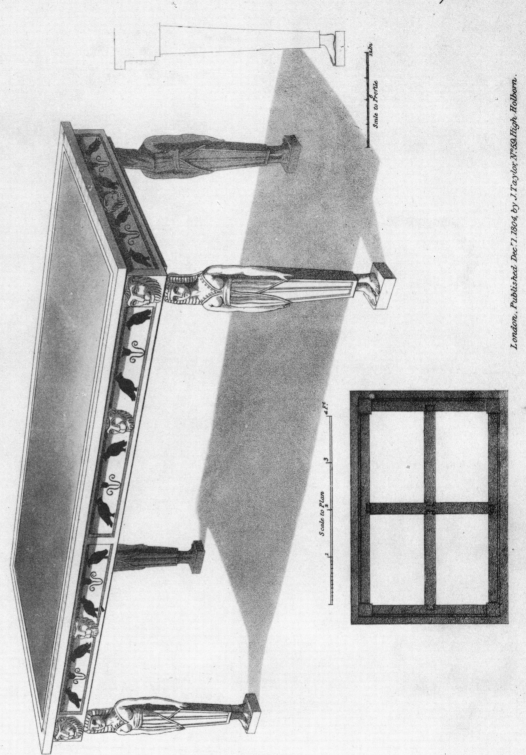

Library Table

Pl __ 88

Scale to Profile

Scale to Plan

London. Published Decr 1. 1804. by J.Taylor N.^o59.High Holborn.

c

Pl. 89

C

Library Table.

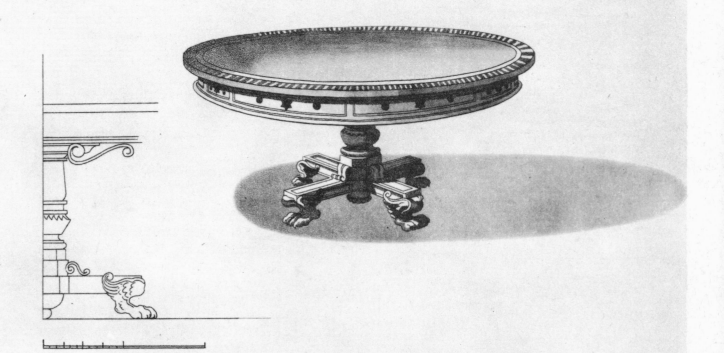

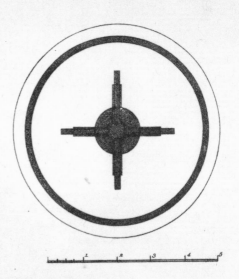

London, Published July 1.1805, by J.Taylor, No 59, High Holborn.

Plate 90.

Dumb Waiters.

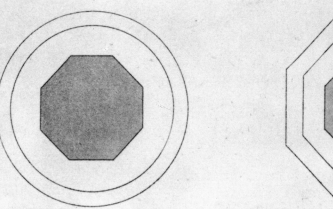

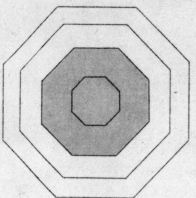

London, Published Jan.ʸ 1ˢᵗ 1807, by J. Taylor, 59, High Holborn.

Pl. 91.

Legs for Sideboards.

London, Published July 1. 1805, by J. Taylor, No. 59, High Holborn.

Pl. 92

Design for a Sideboard.

London. Published Dec.r 1.1804. by J.Taylor. N.o 59 High Holborn.

Design for a Sideboard.

Pl. 93

London. Published Dec.r 1. 1804. by J. Taylor. N.o 59 High Holborn.

Pl.94.

Design for a Sideboard.

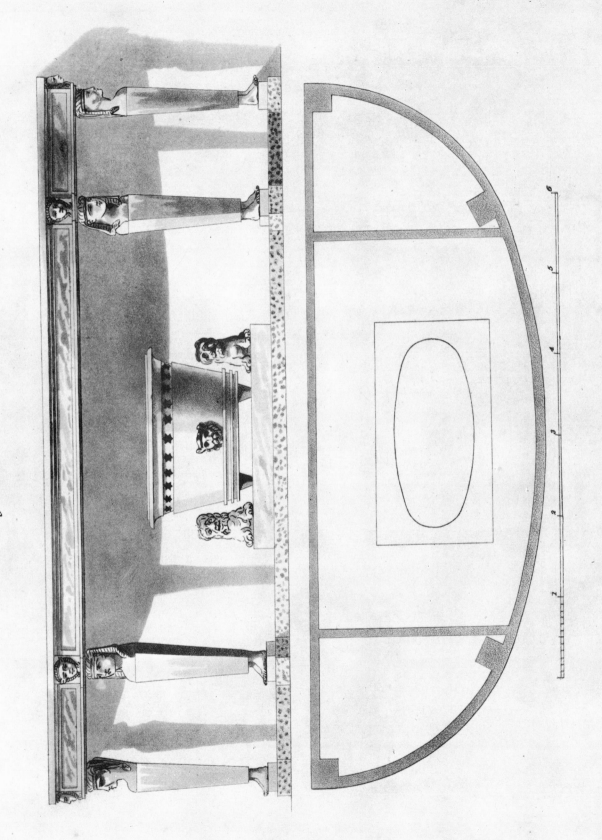

London. Published July 1. 1805, by J.Taylor, No.59, High Holborn.

Pl. 95.

Design for a Side Board.

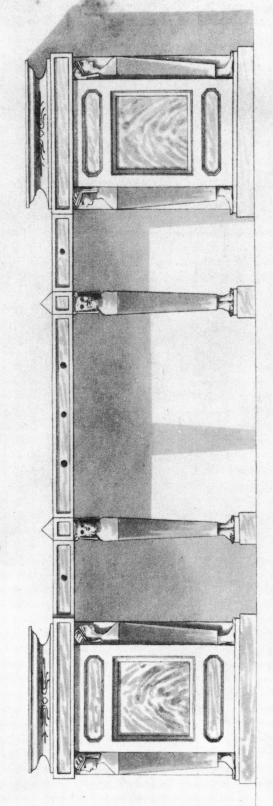

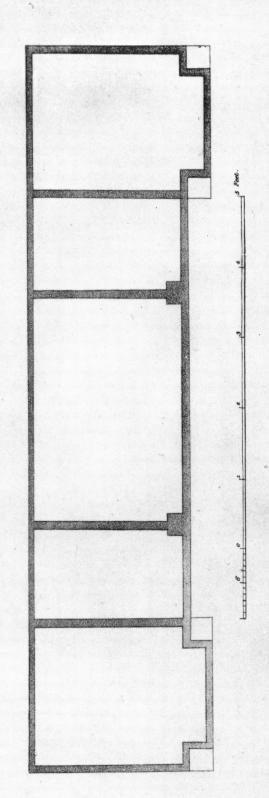

3 Feet.

London. Published July 1. 1805, by J. Taylor, Nº 59, High Holborn.

Pl. 96.

Pedestals for Sideboards.

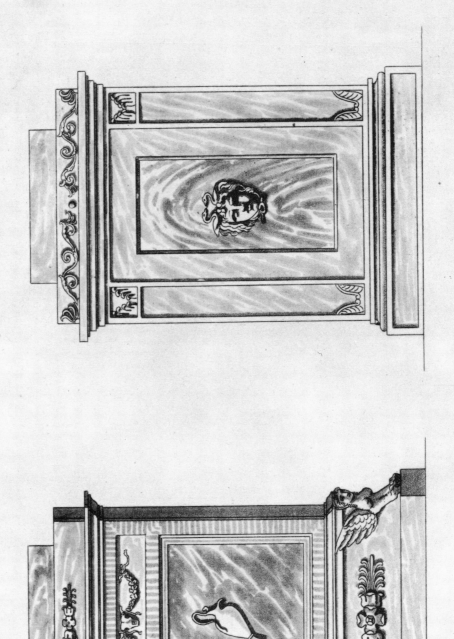

London, Published July 1. 1805. by J.Taylor, N.º59, High Holborn.

Plate 97.

Celleret & Wine-cistern, in the Gothic style.

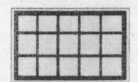

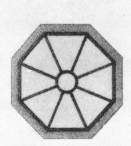

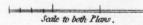

Scale to both Plans.

London, Published Dec.r 1.st 1806, by J. Taylor, 59, High Holborn.

A

Pl 98

Celeretts.

London. Published Dec.r 1.1804, by J.Taylor, N.o 59 High Holborn.

Pl. 99

A

Bookcase.

London Published July 1.1805. by J.Taylor, Nº.59, High Holborn.

Plate 100.

Cylinder Desk and Bookcase.

London, Published Jan.ʳ 1.ˢᵗ 1807, by J. Taylor, 59, High Holborn.

Plate 101.

Secretaire Desk and Bookcase.

London, Published Jan.ʳ 1ˢᵗ 1807, by J.Taylor, 59, High Holborn.

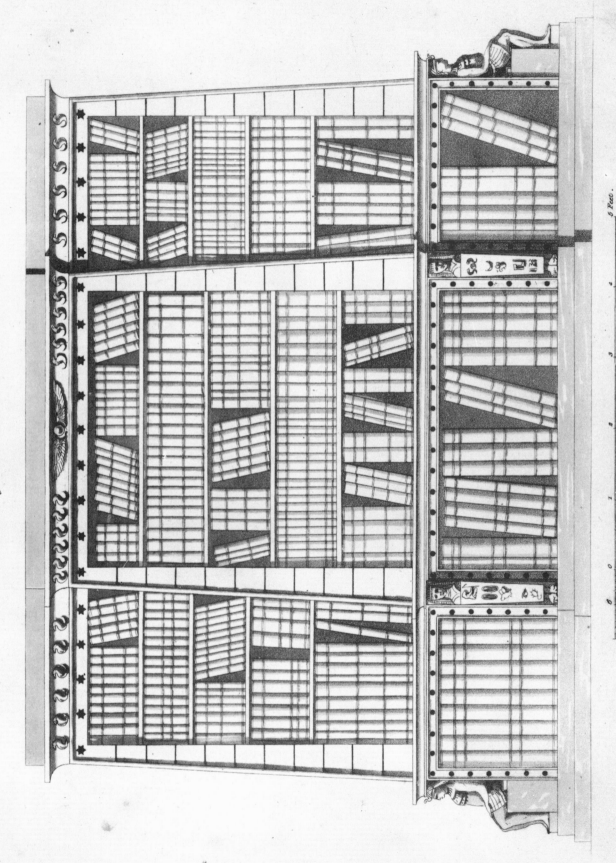

Pl 102.

Library Bookcase.

London. Published July 1.1805. by J Taylor, N.°.59. High Holborn.

5 Feet.

Plate 103.

Library Bookcase.

London, Published Jan.ʳʸ 1.ˢᵗ 1807, by J. Taylor, 59, High Holborn.

B

A

HOMER

VIRGL

Dwarf Library Bookcase.

London. Published Dec. 7. 1804. by J. Taylor, No. 59 High Holborn.

Pl. 104

Plate 105.

Dwarf Book Case.

London. Published Dec.r 1.st 1806, by J. Taylor, 59. High Holborn.

Plate 106.

Gothic.

Book case Doors.

Egyptian.

Chinese.

London, Published Jan.ʸ 1.ˢᵗ 1807, by J. Taylor, 59. High Holborn.

Bookcase Doors

London, Published July 1. 1805, by J. Taylor, Nᵒ. 59. High Holborn.

Pl 108

Screens.

London. Published Dec.r 1, 1804, by J. Taylor, N.o 59 High Holborn.

Pl. 109

B

Fire Screens.

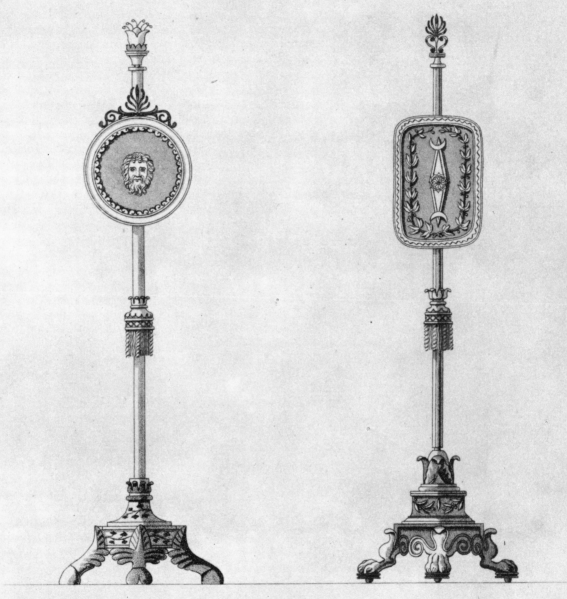

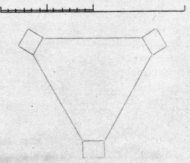

London Published, Dec.r 1.1804, by J Taylor, N.º 59, High Holborn

London, Published Dec.ʳ 1ˢᵗ 1806, by J. Taylor, 59, High Holborn.

Pl. 111.

Tripod Stands for Work Tables, Screens, & Candelabri.

London. Published, July, 1. 1805, by J Taylor, No.59, High Holborn.

Pl. 112

B

Drawing Room Candelabri.

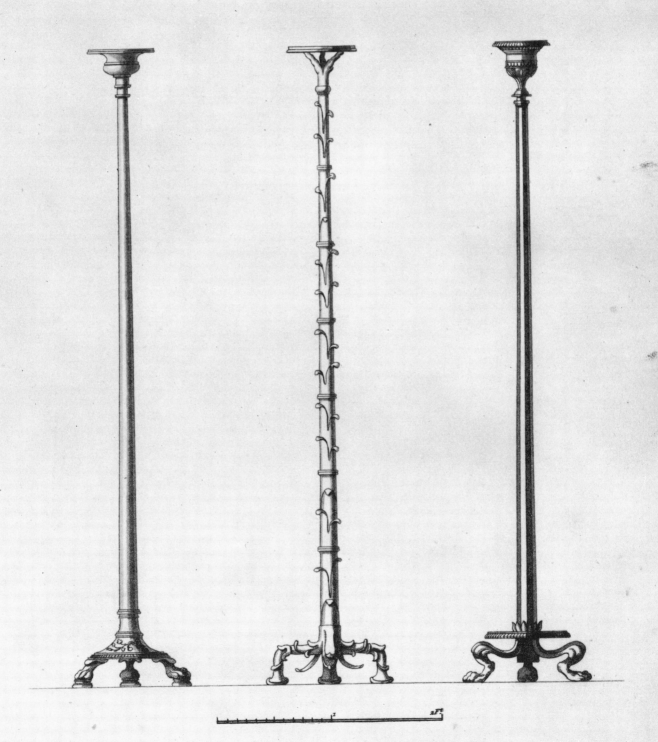

London. Published, Dec.ʳ 1.1804, by J. Taylor, N.º 59. High Holborn.

Pl. 113

A

Drawing Room Candelabri.

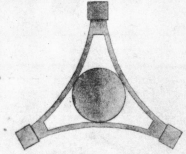

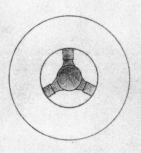

London. Published Dec.r 1. 1804. by J. Taylor. N.o 59 High Holborn.

London, Published Jan.ʳ 1ˢᵗ 1807, by J.Taylor, 59, High Holborn.

Pl 115

Chiffonier.

Scale for Plan.

1   2   3 ft.

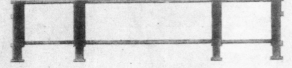

Scale for Profile.

Pier Commode.

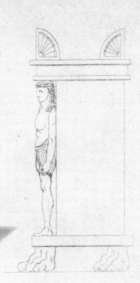

1   2   3 ft.

London. Published Dec.r 1. 1804. by J. Taylor. N.o 59 High Holborn.

Plate 116.

Book shelf and Brackets.

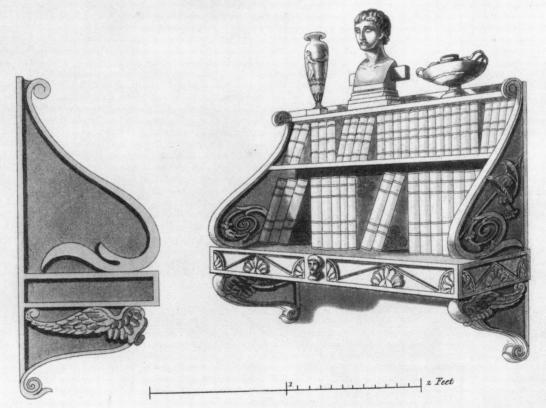

2 Feet

London, Published Dec.r 1.st 1806, by J. Taylor, N.o 59, High Holborn.

Pl.117.

Drawing Room Commodes.

London. Published July 1.1805, by J.Taylor, Nº 59, High Holborn.

Pl. 118

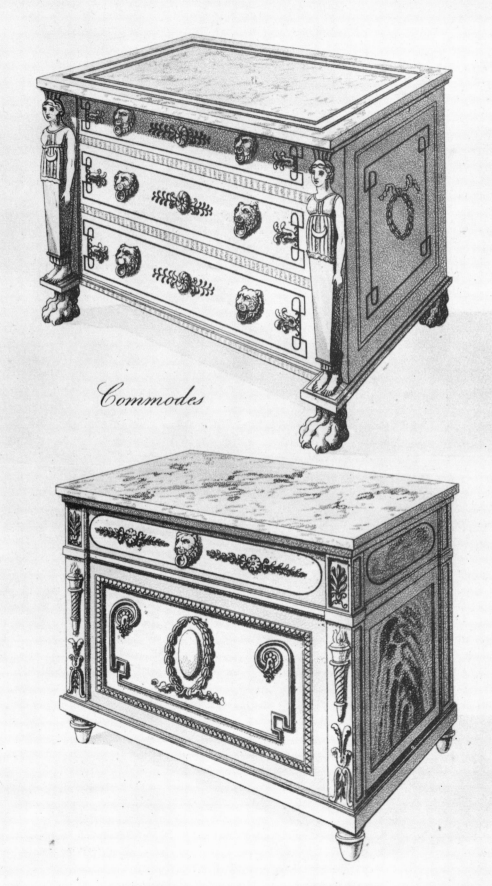

Commodes

London. Publish'd Decr 1. 1804. by J. Taylor. N.º 59 High Holborn.

Commode for Drawing room.

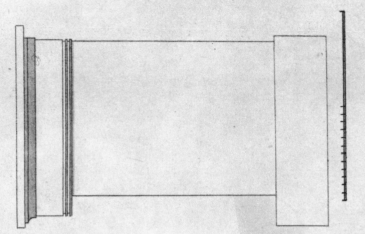

by J. Taylor, N.º 59 High Holborn.

London Published Dec.ʳ 1. 1804.

Pl. 120

Pier Table
and Glass.

Scale for Elevation.

Scale for Plan.

London. Published Dec.r 1. 1804, by J. Taylor, N.o 59 High Holborn.

Console Tables.

Pl. 121.

London. Published Dec.r 1. 1804, by J. Taylor N.o 59 High Holborn.

Plate 122.

Drawing Room Pier Table.

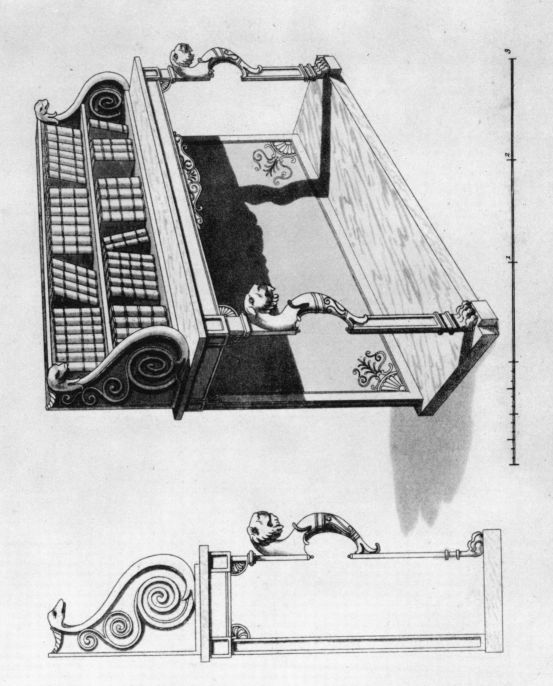

London, Published Dec.r 1.st 1806, by J. Taylor, N.o 59, High Holborn.

Pl.123.

Escrotore.

London. Published July 1.1805, by J.Taylor, N°59, High Holborn.

Pl 124.

Escrotore.

Pl. 125

B

Cheval Dressing Glass.

London, Published July 1. 1805, by J. Taylor, Nᵒ 59, High Holborn.

Pl. 126.

C

Cheval Dressing Glass.

London, Published July 1. 1805, by J. Taylor, No. 59, High Holborn.

Pl. 127

Cheval Dressing Glass.

London. Published Decr. 1. 1804, by J. Taylor, N.° 59 High Holborn.

Pl. 128.

Bason Stands.

London, Published July 1. 1805, by J. Taylor, N° 59, High Holborn.

Pl. 129

Night Tables

London. Published. Dec.r 1. 1804. by J. Taylor. N.o 59. High Holborn.

Pot Cupboards

Pl 130

London. Published Dec.r 1.1804. by I.Taylor, N.o 59. High Holborn.

Plate 137.

Double Chest of Drawers

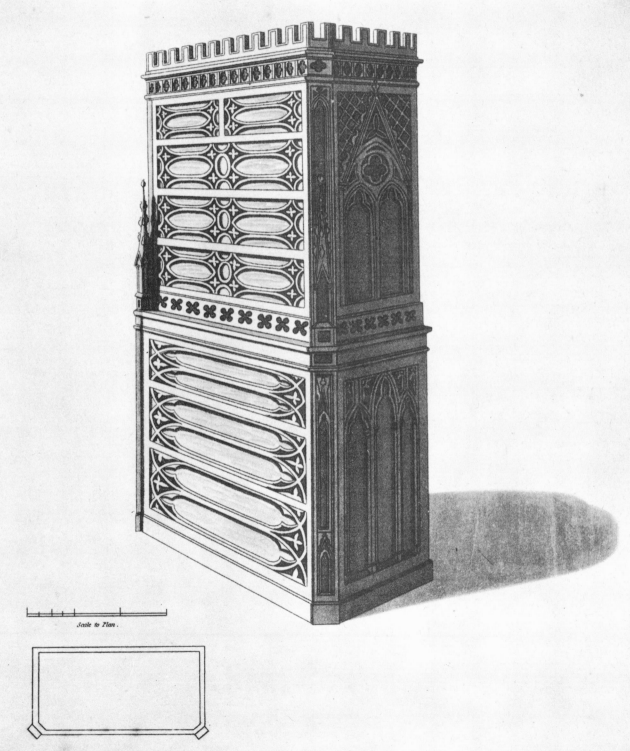

Scale to Plan.

London, Published Jany 1st 1807, by J.Taylor, 59, High Holborn.

Plate 132

Ladies Wardrobe.

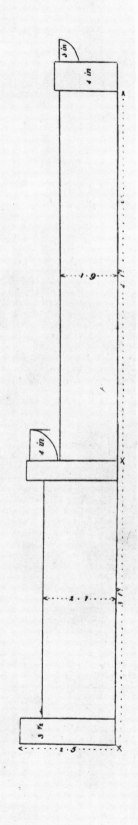

London. Published Dec.r 1. 1804, by J.Taylor, N.o59 High Holborn .

Pl. 133.

Wardrobe.

London, Published July 1, 1805, by J. Taylor, Nº 59, High Holborn.

Plate 134.

Dwarf Wardrobe

London, Published Dec.ʳ 1ᵗʰ 1806, by J. Taylor, 59. High Holborn.

Pl. 135

Mirror.

A

London. Published, Dec.ʳ 1.1804, by J.Taylor, N.º 59, High Holborn.

Pl 136

B

Mirror

London. Published, Decr 1.1804, by J.Taylor, N.º 59, High Holborn.

Pl. 137.

Chandelier.

London. Published July 1.1805, by J.Taylor, N°.59.High Holborn.

Pl.138.

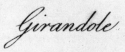

Girandole

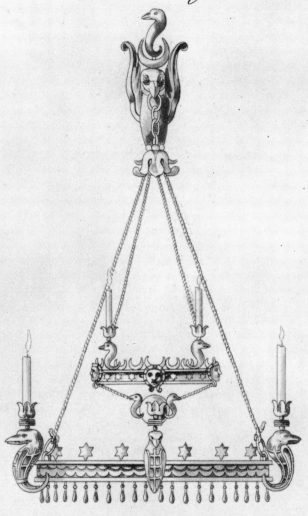

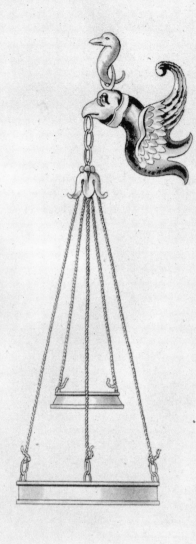

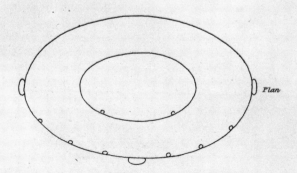

Plan

London, Published July 1.1805, by J. Taylor, No 59, High Holborn.

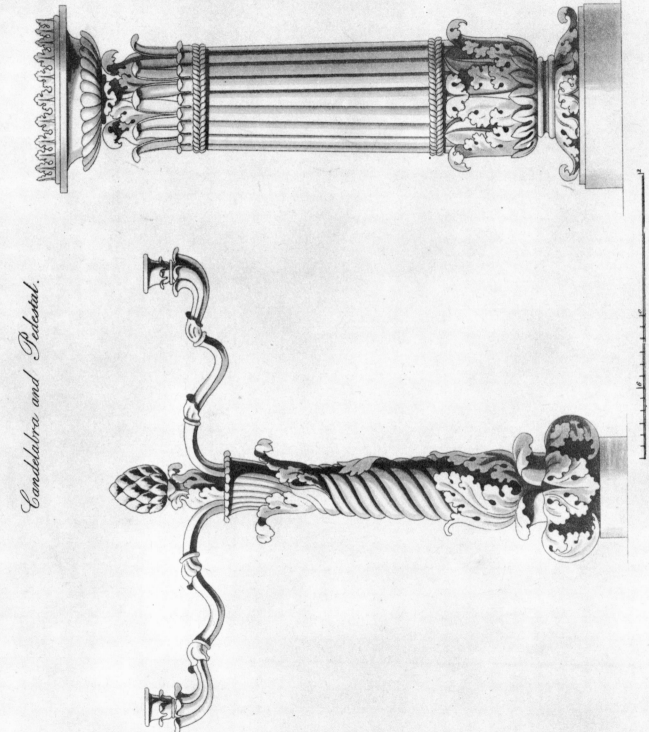

Plate 139.

Candelabra and Pedestal.

London, Published Jan.ᵃ 1.ˢᵗ 1807, by J. Taylor, 59, High Holborn.

Plate 140.

Chandelier.

London, Published Jan^{ry} 1st 1807, by J. Taylor, 59, High Holborn.

Pl. 141.

Girandole, Vases & Candlesticks.

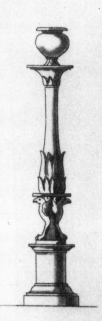

London, Published July 1.1805, by J.Taylor, No 59, High Holborn.

Pl 142

Pedestals for Statues, Busts, &c.

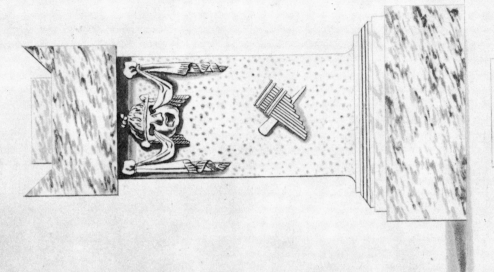

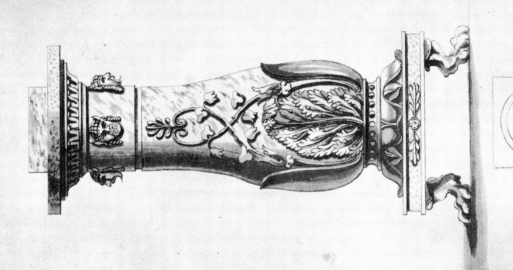

12 ft

London. Published Dec.r 1. 1804. by J. Taylor. N.o 59 High Holborn.

Pl.143.

Jardinieres.

London. Published July 1.1805, by J.Taylor, N°59, High Holborn.

Pl. 144.

Stand for Flowers &c.

London. Published, July 1, 1808, by J. Taylor, N.º 59, High Holborn.

London. Published Dec.ʳ 1. 1804, by J. Taylor, N.º 59 High Holborn.

Pl 146

London. Published Dec.ᵗ 1.1804, by J.Taylor, Nº 59 High Holborn.

London Published, Dec.r 1.1804, by J. Taylor, N.o 59, High Holborn.

D

Chimney Glass & Decorations.

London. Published, Dec.r 1.1804, by J.Taylor. N.o 59. High Holborn.

Pl. 149

Plate 149.

Decoration for a Drawing Room in the Chinese taste.

London, Published Jan.1.st 1807. by J. Taylor, 59. High Holborn.

20 Feet.

Pl. 150

Plate 150.

Drawing Room Decoration in the gothic style.

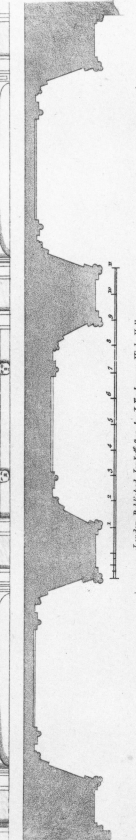

London. Published Jan.ʳ 1.ˢᵗ 1807. by J. Taylor, 59. High Holborn.

Boudoir with Ottomans.

London.Published.Dec.7.1804.by.I.Taylor, N.º59.High Holborn.

Plate 152.

State Drawing Room, shewing its Decorations and Furniture.

Pl 152

London, Published Jan.ʳ 1ˢᵗ 1827, by J. Taylor, 59, High Holborn.

Pl. 153

Plate 153.

Section and Plan of a State Drawing Room.

Sofa

Table

Sofa

Sofa

Sofa

Table

State Escort.

Table

Music Escort.

Music Escort.

b

b

a a a Chairs.

b b b Candelabri.

c c c F. Seats.

London, Published Jan.t 1.st 1820, by J. Taylor, 59, High Holborn.

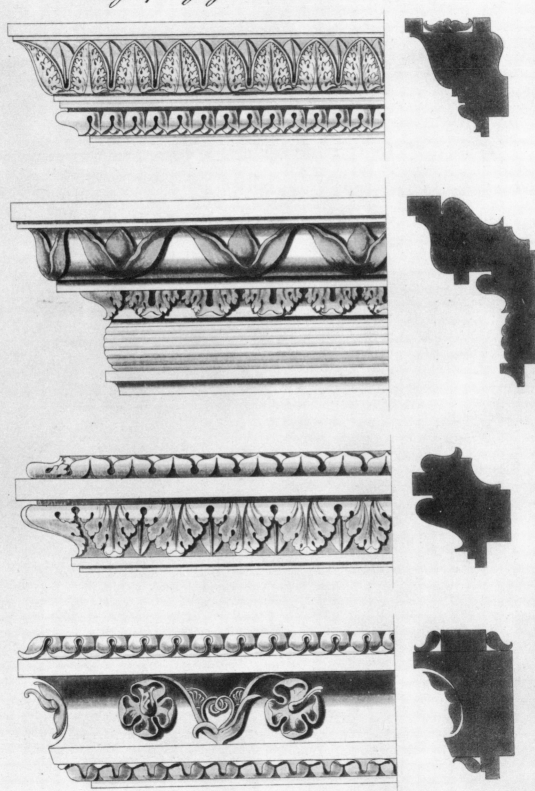

London, Published Dec.r 1.st 1806, by J.Taylor, 59, High Holborn.

Plate 155.

Glass Frames.

London, Published Dec.r 1.st 1806, by J.Taylor. 59, High Holborn.

Plate 156.

Large Moldings for Cabinet work, full size.

London, Published Jan.ʳ 1ˢᵗ 1807, by J. Taylor, 59, High Holborn.

Plate 157.

Small Moldings for Cabinet work.

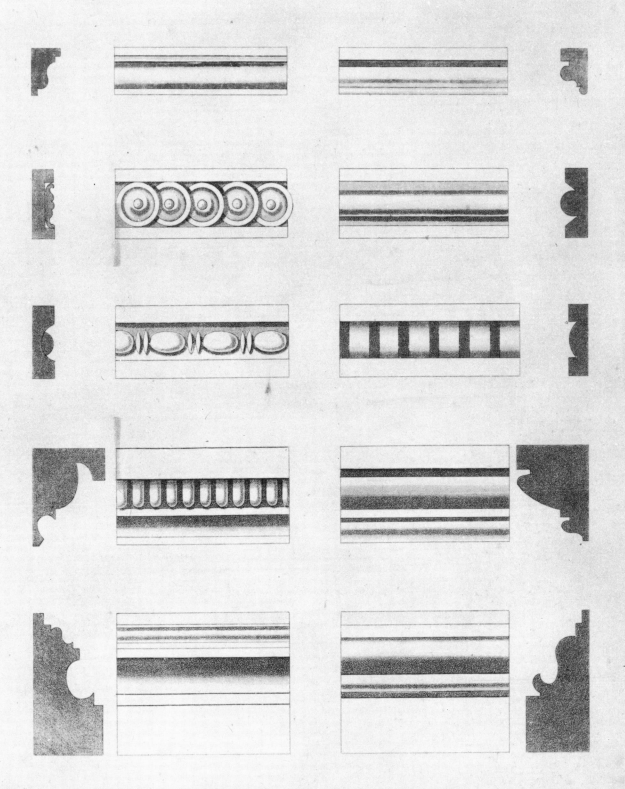

London, Published Jan.ʳ 1ˢᵗ 1807, by J. Taylor, 59, High Holborn.

Plate 158.

Fretts.

London, Published Jan.ʳ 1ˢᵗ 1807, by J. Taylor, 59, High Holborn.